# Louis' Place

*Taming the Bush...*

*Making and Selling Canadian Electronics...*

*Creating Something from Nothing.*

The Story of Louis Potvin

From Bonnyville to Lillooet Lake via Tokyo and Havana

As told to Ron Rose

Printed in Victoria, Canada

**Canadian Cataloguing in Publication Data**

Potvin, Louis, 1924–
    Louis' place

    ISBN 1-55212-293-X

    1. Potvin, Louis, 1924-   2. Prairie Provinces--Biography.
3. Radio broadcasters--Biography.   I. Rose, Ron, 1919-
II. Title.
FC601.P64A3 1999        920.71      C99-911140-X
F1034.3.P67A3 1999

# TRAFFORD

This book was published *on-demand* in cooperation with Trafford Publishing.
On-demand publishing is a unique process and service of making a book available for retail sale to the public taking advantage of on-demand manufacturing and Internet marketing. **On-demand publishing** includes promotions, retail sales, manufacturing, order fulfilment, accounting and collecting royalties on behalf of the author.

Suite 6E, 2333 Government St., Victoria, B.C. V8T 4P4, CANADA
Phone      250-383-6864        Toll-free   1-888-232-4444 (Canada & US)
Fax        250-383-6804        E-mail      sales@trafford.com
Web site   www.trafford.com    TRAFFORD PUBLISHING IS A DIVISION OF TRAFFORD HOLDINGS LTD.
Trafford Catalogue #99-0045    www.trafford.com/robots/99-0045.html

10      9      8      7      6      5      4      3      2

# DEDICATION

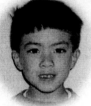

My wife Carol and I offer this
book to our grandchildren in the
hope they will find it *amusant*
and even learn something from
the recollections of an old man
who has lived quite a lot.

*Bonne chance* Renée, Douglas,
Jacqueline, Kevin, Rosemary,
Marianne, Gillian, Michael,
Ross, Alexander, Marc, Mireille.

*Louis Potvin*

# *Acknowledgments*

We owe a debt of gratitude to countless
people who have guided this journey into
the past in many ways. They know who
they are. Specifically we appreciate the
common sense of two good-humoured
women, Carol Potvin and Hélène Mooney,
whose forbearance made it possible;
the expertise and insight of Alex Rose,
who made some sensible suggestions;
our demon designer, Lorne Craig, whose
cover painting, chapter title drawings and
parcelling did so much for the book; and
Trafford Publishing, who introduced us to the
marvels of electronic publishing.

LP and RR

## *About Ron Rose*

Co-author Ron Rose began an unlikely association with Louis Potvin 30 years ago and this book has been incubating since then. A reporter and editor with the Vancouver Sun in its heyday of chronicling the vagaries of B.C., he covered the Legislature from the time of W.A.C. Bennett through Dave Barrett, Bill Bennett, and Bill Vander Zalm.

He created The Sun's Indian beat– making it the first paper in Western Canada to take a serious look at aboriginal hopes and problems.

# CONTENTS

# Preface

This book has been some 30 years in the making. At least it's that long since the idea first occurred to us, then took shape in fits and starts.

I remember Louis and I were out on Lillooet Lake, one long summer evening, in his 12-foot aluminum boat – his beachcombing boat, he called it – trailing green sedges and black gnats and fighting off more sockeye fry than we caught trout.

I'd started going up there weekends, because my youngest son Tony was working for him during the high school holidays, learning the arts of taming the bush.

The place was magic – a serene haven in a sunlit bowl of snowcapped mountains.

There wouldn't be a sound except the putter of the outboard until something would remind him of a story. There'd be another story around the next point, and sometimes there would be reflections on radio communications, or dodging clouds while flying in and out of coastal inlets, or how to keep a business from going broke, or how to be a salesman or how to make something out of nothing.

"You should write a book," I found myself exclaiming.

I, as a newspaper writer, must have promised to help him, because we kept talking about it on other visits over the years as he continued the improvements that turned the soldier's settlement he bought for $1,500 into a recreational subdivision and country estate.

And finally, I got him to start jotting down his recollections in some old school exercise books. Among other things, he has a prodigious memory. It was a long and fascinating struggle for us both to organize it all, but he's a great storyteller, as you will see.

Over to you, Louis....


Ron Rose

# INTRODUCTION

Sunday drivers who venture onto the logging road down Lillooet Lake from Pemberton may wonder what's behind the Heather Jean Properties sign on a woodland trail leading to the lake. And I've heard people asking, whoever could be running the place?

Well, I'll tell you about him. About me, that is.

I have come to rest (more or less) in this splendid isolation after a lifetime of hard work, false starts, disappointments, brazen gall and good luck.

Looking back at the age of 76, I see the silhouettes of a number of people, all of them me at various stages in my life. I see a shy young boy, brought up in a hard-scrabble farming community in rural Alberta, his first words French, his English learned painstakingly at school.

I see a lost kid, moved to Vancouver with his parents, living in downtown rooms while his father got work in what

11

seemed a glamorous job as a stool pigeon for the Vancouver police department.

I remember a quick move to the hinterland of Port Coquitlam, when it turned out that there were a lot of nasty people in the big city who didn't like stool pigeons.

I remember us all dabbling at anything that would put food on the table in those Depression years, and later, learning radio at a business school, in what would be the road to my future. As a teenager I operated my own little radio repair business.

Later came enlistment in the Royal Canadian Air Force and training as a wireless operator-radio technician, finally a real job in the developing radiotelephone business, and successive careers as an international salesman, property developer and commercial broadcaster.

All these recollections flip past like the pages of a calendar turning in one of those old movies.

One of the projects I take pride in is Mountain FM Radio, which I set up to tie together the three isolated communities of Squamish, Whistler and Pemberton..

It went on the air in 1981, after three years of research, CRTC applications and hearings. It was the first radio station in an area where AM reception was difficult and it promoted the "Sea to Sky Country" corridor, a name trumpeted by the Squamish Chamber of Commerce to identify the area in the public mind.

My wife Carol and I got a real charge out of running the

station from a studio in Squamish, and figure we did some good. Its road reports from repeater stations in the area became the guide to motorists negotiating the changing and dangerous conditions on the road to Whistler.

In those days, rockslides and washouts were common on what was dubbed the Killer Highway to Squamish. Squamish commerce depended on an open road and on Thursdays and Fridays there was a build-up of ski traffic to Whistler. So it became a must to tune Mountain FM at Horseshoe Bay before beginning on the winding road.

Later we put in four more repeater stations to expand Mountain FM's reach to Gibsons, Sechelt, Pender Harbour and Egmont. We learned a lot about the communities that way. They learned about each other.

Our lake property began as a holiday retreat, and gradually turned into a mink ranch, sawmill, then a resort subdivision.

I had to be a beachcomber, a sawmill-planermill operator, landscaper, house builder, strata council manager. I had to generate my own electricity through a Pelton wheel in one of the creeks and pipe mountain water for people in the subdivision that took shape. There were no telephones out in the bush so I had to rig my own UHF link to the outside phone service.

I found myself having to hire bulldozer operators, carpenters, welders, electricians, plumbers, some living in the area and others who came in to do jobs. At one time we had a bunkhouse and cookhouse for seasonal workers.

I learned the intricacies of dealing with government and municipal bureaucrats, and learned the vagaries of public opinion.

Repeatedly during my adult life, I have had to re-learn the lessons of my Depression-era childhood: that you have to work to survive, and work hard, even when the task appears hopeless.

I survived dangerous flights to upcoast installations (once I was left on a mountaintop only to find my return flight had been diverted on a rescue mission and crashed into the sea while lost in the fog, killing all aboard).

I somehow became a sales executive in a company that was struggling in a shrinking marketplace, and managed to get Canadian government support for international sales trips to Japan, Latin America and Cuba.

I met Fidel Castro and declined an invitation to get better acquainted with the Cuban revolution against the capitalist system, although I managed to sell them a million dollars' worth of radio equipment, travelling there repeatedly over a three-year period.

I told Sony in Japan I couldn't use their experimental transistor radio or their round, early-model cathode tube television screen, and it was only later that I realized we weren't big enough to handle their tremendous breakthrough in electronics.

But I did some things right. I managed to survive the

stresses of business success and the responsibilities of a growing family. I coped with the death of my first wife Jean after 30 years of marriage. I watched my son and daughter grow up and come to grips with the vicissitudes of life. And I found peace with my second wife, Carol, who has helped me for 25 years and has become my manager in the best sense.

Together we keep busy in our lakeside home and watch our grandchildren mature and try to help them prepare for whatever happens next.

Louis Potvin

*Veil or Caul, n.*

*Plain part at back of a woman's cap; membrane enclosing foetus; portion of this occas. found on child's head (good omen & charm against drowning.)*
- *The Concise Oxford Dictionary*
*Fifth Edition*

# Chapter One
## Prairie Life

I entered the world with a veil over my head, in Bonnyville, Alberta, July 19, 1924. The veil, or caul, is a membrane that has to be removed promptly at birth to prevent suffocation. In older times, such an event was considered to bring good fortune, and considerable sums of money were paid for a veil or part thereof; they being sought by sea captains.

When I became frustrated as a child, my mother would say, "Don't worry, Petit Louis, you were born with a veil over your head and things will work out for you." I suppose one could interpret this as instilling positive thinking.

I have thought of this at various times of my life, when I have escaped drowning or had good luck that got me through difficult times. Once I visited the Nantucket Whaling Museum on the U.S. Atlantic seaboard and saw the pocket-sized boxes used by whaling captains as late as the 1890s to safeguard their lucky pieces of veil.

My mother was 17 and my father 32. Opportunities were limited in this mostly French-Canadian grain-farming community of 500, so her marriage to the postmaster and town notary was looked upon with favour. After one year of marriage, my parents sought greater opportunity, so they moved to Vancouver, B.C.

Work was hard to come by, but my father found employment as a stool pigeon for the city police. His job was to be served drinks in the various speakeasies and later re-enter the premises with a uniformed police officer and lay charges. This job put food on the table but came to an end when he was told by the bad guys his life would be endangered if he continued. So he left the force.

In 1928 my parents moved to Port Coquitlam, started a small farming operation and sold produce at the New Westminster farmers' market. I was kind of in the way of this new business venture, so it was decided after several years that I should be shipped out to stay for one year with my grandparents, Napoleon and Desneiges Marcoux, in Bonnyville.

## Travels with my Aunt

I traveled by train to Edmonton with my 21-year-old Aunt Yvonne, my mother's sister, who had spent the summer with us. Aunt Yvonne, a school-teacher, was being pursued by the 60-year-old CNR station agent in Bonnyville, a relationship that was off again, on again, with my grandparents objecting strongly. But my grandparents were finally persuaded to consent to the marriage.

*Duclos Hospital building, standing deserted in 1983 in the centre of a Bonnyville wheat field. First a farmhouse, it was converted to a hospital by Reverend Duclos of the United Church. It was here in 1924 that I became the first child of our rebel Catholic group to be born into the United Church.*

The old boy had grown children in their 20s and 30s as well as a 10- and 12-year-old still at home. He had lost his wife some time back. My young aunt and I rode the CNR coach to Edmonton, where we were met by her future husband.

The next day they were hurriedly married in a big, empty, cold church. Aunt Yvonne's sister, my Aunt Rosa, who was 15 at the time, was also in attendance.

On our way to Bonnyville, a waiter asked my 60-year-old new Uncle Joe if he could get anything more for his daughter. The old boy replied, "That's my wife." We were traveling fancy in my uncle's new Buick sedan, which drew many a glance as we passed the horse-drawn wagons along the dirt roads.

At dark we arrived at a farm owned by acquaintances of

21

Uncle Joe. Not expecting us, they were astonished at the marriage. But, this being the honeymoon night, we were put up in the attic. Two beds separated by a few feet, with a white sheet hung on a rope between the beds for privacy.

We undressed in our compartments in the dim light of a hand-carried coal oil lamp. The newlyweds bedded down on one side of the sheet, my 15-year-old aunt and I on the other side. It wasn't long before the old boy was bursting at the seams. We could hear many protests as the old goat forced himself upon his new bride. The crying went on until the event ended. And then it was repeated later that night!

At the age of nine, I didn't know what to think, but having lived on a farm, I had some grasp of what had occurred. My 15-year-old aunt made me promise not to talk about this to anyone, and until now my lips have been sealed. At breakfast, we told our hosts we had a wonderful rest.

I looked out the car windows as we traveled on, and saw the farms were getting further and further apart and the landscape more bleak and lonely. We arrived at my grandparents' place, by a small lake void of trees except for a distant patch that stood alone. It was barren compared to the coast and this added to my feelings of loneliness.

But it wasn't long before I felt at home again. The next morning my grandfather Napoleon took me out to the storage shed to retrieve his father's cap and overcoat for me. My great-grandfather's name was Pierre Marcoux. He was born around 1836 in Quebec, and had died in 1928 at the Bonnyville farm. My grandfather lifted the hat off the nail on which it was hanging, removed a handful of baby mice from inside the cap, slapped it a couple of times on his leg to dislodge the mouse bedding and said: "This will keep you warm, Louis; it even has ear flaps you can pull down in winter."

The long, heavy coat was also given a good shake. Grandmother Desneiges, a good seamstress, as all women had to be in those days, laid out the coat, traced the proper size and cut it down to fit her "Petit Louis," as I was called, little Louis. I felt her warmth and love, a feeling that I have carried with me all my life.

*Loius, age 10, wearing Great-Grandfather's cut-down coat and hat on the farm in Bonnyville, Alberta, 1934.*

As I settled in, I soon was speaking French again. My 15-year-old aunt showed me the way to school. I was introduced to my teacher Henri Bourgoin, a second cousin through marriage. Henri had come to Bonnyville in the late 1920s as a missionary graduate from Montreal. He was informed I had failed grade three at Central School in Port Coquitlam, and would be repeating the grade. It would not have made much difference if I had moved into grade four. The one-room rural schoolhouse had around 30 students from grades one to eight, the older students helping teach the younger ones. A very difficult job for a teacher. For me this was a regressive step, but the experience benefited me in other ways that would not become apparent until years later.

The school complex — residential school home, field hospital, church and supporting farm – was run by the newly formed United Church which had promised to help the French-Canadian Protestants and others who were no longer following the Catholic Church. Henri's life was a spartan one in those Depression days, living on a teacher's salary of $10 a month with not much help from the outside.

My daily walk to and from school in all weather brought me close to nature. The howling winds at times would blow the snow over the fence posts, my only signposts, and I had to have my wits about me. Some days were so cold that three pairs of stockings and moccasins could not keep my feet warm. The scarf wrapped around my face became a frosty beard.

The school outhouse had a 2-by-4 board over a pit, and the board developed a yellowed-ice build-up. It was here I learned how to do my business without sitting down. Eaton's catalogue was on hand, the affordable toilet paper of the day.

Obtaining drinking water involved filling a porcelain crock at the nearby well. The pail at the well was attached to a rope through a pulley and had to be banged down a few times to break the ice and fill the bucket. A porcelain-covered tin cup hung on the wall beside the water container. Each student took the cup, poured a drink and replaced it carefully.

From use, the porcelain had chipped away from the edge of the cup. I soon came down with impetigo, which bled, crusted over and cracked open again and again. I, along with many other students, suffered this ailment because we all drank from the same cup, and it was not until I returned to the B.C. coast that I found an ointment that made this disappear. I did not feel any neglect as everybody suffered some ailment in those days, in that environment, and only life-threatening matters were cause for medical attention.

The long winter nights at the farm were passed playing a popular card game called 500. My illiterate grandfather excelled at this game and so did I. My grandmother and my young aunt hooked rugs. They strung a piece of burlap within a frame and cut any old coloured clothing into long strips. They sketched a scene on the burlap and hooked in

*Grandfather and Grandmother Marcoux and their six children (left to right): Back: Arsene (Bill), Rosa, Alma (my mother), Albert. Front: Lena, Grandfather Napoleon, Grandmother Desneiges, Yvonne. Grandfather was an unschooled philosopher and my mentor when I was a young boy.*

the rag pieces with a tool made by my grandfather out of a nail, filed to shape and fitted into a wooden handle. The rugs were used for years and felt warm over the cold floors.

Relatives and friends would gather at times for a hoe-down. It was exciting to hear the horses and sleighs arrive for the party, some with bells a-tinkling. The depth of our warmth and affection for these visitors is something you no longer see. Isolation and hardships created the need for human contact.

If it was available, wine would flow, but wine or not, the tap-dancing would start to the sound of one or more violins. The older folk spoke in French about the Quebec they had left some 20 years earlier to open up new land for themselves. The next generation talked about local matters in both French and English, and of better opportunities in British Columbia. But too soon it was time for the visitors to go home, harness up the horses that had been covered and fed, place the hot irons under the covers in the sleigh and head off under the star-covered sky.

During the harsh winter months, my 55-year-old grandfather would become restless, pacing the floor. No radio, no magazines or newspapers, only the pictures in Eaton's catalogue. Most evenings he would take down a bag of peanuts from the top of the cupboard, place a small handful on the table for himself and reluctantly put two or three peanuts out for me. He would look at my meagre portion as he put the bag away, hesitate and most times add one peanut to my allotment. In spite of the philosophical teachings he imparted, he was very frugal and selfish when it came to food, relating it to the effort it took to produce it.

## Watching Wheat Grow

The spring thaw came, the fields were made bare, the ploughing begun. Wheat was sown, the rapid growth soon covering the fields with golden waves. Soon the wheat was cut, baled and left lying on the ground. It was hard work stooking, picking up the bundles and piling them in a predetermined style to dry.

My grandfather packed his own shotgun shells, and

some evenings we went out to scare away the ducks that were feasting on the harvested wheat stooks. As we entered the field, the ducks would take off by the hundreds. The shotgun, fired upwards without aim, brought one or more to the ground.

The threshers came with their horse-drawn equipment and tractor, then the hard work began, pitch forking the wheat bundles onto the wagons, then hand forking into the conveyor, which fed the thresher. The threshing machine was powered by a long, wide belt turned by the tractor. It beat the stalks to separate the chaff, the grain flowing out into an empty wagon and the exhaust pipe blowing straw into a large pile.

When the wagon was full of grain, off it went, horse-drawn, to one of the four grain elevators by the railroad tracks. Cooking and baking for the crew, who slept overnight, was a big job. Some of the harvesters could eat a whole pie at one sitting.

School was out in late June and I was informed I had passed. I might as well have entered grade four instead of repeating grade three as both grades seemed to receive the same level of instruction.

The gopher plague was on, and the government paid a bounty of one cent per gopher tail. I trapped my gophers by filling a barrel with lake water, loading the barrel on a horse-drawn stone boat and filling the gopher holes with a hose from the barrel. The gophers would eventually pop out to escape drowning, the dog anxiously awaiting their appearance. There were so many gophers that my trapping did not reduce the number very much. I did however have a bag full of gopher tails to sell. This bounty was later dropped, when the gopher population came to be viewed in a different light.

## Back and Forth

*The Potvin Port Coquitlam home in 1928. It was here that parents Alma and Alfred raised chickens and grew produce. Port Coquitlam had been subdivided as an overseas land promotion when it was expected to be the Western Terminus of the Canadian Pacific Railway. The dream died when the railway went right on by. The area remained mostly small farm holdings albeit with piped water and a grid of boardwalks.*

Summer over now, at 10 years old, I was placed on the train alone, destination New Westminster. I was a little apprehensive but arrived okay the next day.

My mother and father met the train and away we went to our Port Coquitlam farm in our 1928 sedan, cut down into a one-seater pick-up. I soon observed tension between my parents; they were not speaking to each other and were very curt with me. I realized the relationship had deteriorated considerably.

The next day, a moving van came and loaded our few household goods. Our new $15-per-month rented home was near Nanaimo and Hastings streets in Vancouver's east end.

*In the garden with father Alfred who was a misfit in the agricultural world. Serving as a Coquitlam trustee and baseball umpire, he also won a $500 Grand Prize for formulating English crossword puzzles although his mother tongue was French.*

My mother had entered into a business arrangement with a partner, renting a produce stall at Blackburn's Public Market in Vancouver, selling poultry products, etc. My father was to find work and keep house.

In mid-September 1934 I enrolled in grade four at Hastings School. I enjoyed this school. It had excellent teachers and I remember Mr. Chute as a good principal. I did well in grades four and five and then completed a month and a half of grade six, before being moved back to Bonnyville again. No one took into account the effect this second move would have on my schooling. Of course, being ready for a new adventure, I said nothing that might discourage it.

My mother was anxious to be out of her marriage and the burden of supporting my father. She worked out a plan. Not an easy thing to do in 1936 and it took considerable courage under the circumstances. My mother's brother-in-law, Ernest Gagnon, was visiting from Bonnyville and offered to drive us back there.

While my father was out playing cards one evening, my mother, Aunt Rosa and Uncle Ernest loaded up the 1932 Ford pick-up used in the business and all four of us slipped away. I felt sorry for my father.

## An Epic Ride

We made Hope the first night, the next day the Fraser Canyon and across to Revelstoke, where we planned on taking the ferry down the Arrow Lakes to lower B.C. The ride through the Canyon road was hair-raising in those days, very rough and narrow with no guard rails. The next morning in Revelstoke we found the ferry had just closed down for the winter and we would have to retrace our steps to Kamloops, then go south across B.C. to Calgary.

We drove all night in great discomfort. The road ahead seen through dim headlights was nerve-wracking: gravel, potholes and rolling rocks, which we had to avoid and push off the road.

At 4 a.m. we arrived at the National Park entrance and found the barrier closed. We all dozed off. Early in the morning, a uniformed park warden arrived, lifted the barrier, checked us through and welcomed us to Alberta. We arrived at my grandparents' farm in Bonnyville the afternoon of the next day, thoroughly exhausted. Word spread of our arrival and soon relatives visited to hear about our fascinating trip through the Rockies in three and a half days.

The howling winds of October 1936 reminded me it would soon be cold, very cold. My grandparents, not ones to throw anything out, soon located my overcoat and cap, only this time there were no mice in the cap.

Back at Duclos School, I was warmly welcomed by my former teacher Henri Bourgoin.

"My, how you have grown," he said.

There were enough grade six students to form one small group in the single classroom. There were now a few Cree Metis in my class, some in the school home, some living temporarily in empty farm buildings. There were also girls from the school home. Others, like myself, walked to school daily.

I was a curiosity to my fellow classmates, having come from the big city. I had to describe streetcars, movie theatres, vaudeville shows, and the Rockies. My trading instincts soon surfaced, and I traded some of my city goods to my native friends: my belt with a large buckle, my pocket knife, magnifying glass, photographs. What we called Big Little Books, which contained comics of Popeye, Alice the

32

Goon and Little Orphan Annie, were in great demand. In return, I received beaded Indian moccasins and gloves.

The Indian goods had a pleasant aroma to them, likely due to the smoky conditions they were exposed to in their homes.

My Cree classmates were smart and kept me on my toes. I heard one became a lawyer later in life. English was the language of the classroom. During outdoor noon-hour games, when the weather was mild, Henri, our teacher, would sit on the school steps in his heavy bearskin coat and watch us play. All three languages could be heard, English, French and Cree. I made a pocket notebook and started recording Cree words the Metis boys taught me. I found myself adept at this and it increased our friendship.

I was taught how to catch gophers using a piece of binder twine with a noose on one end. You placed the noose around the gopher hole and waited patiently until the gopher showed himself, then with a quick jerk of the twine, the gopher was caught in the noose. Then you had to twirl the twine around and around, shortening the span each time around until you could grab the gopher.

I did some trapping at the lake for muskrats and a few weasels (ermine), which frequented the chicken coop. I soon learned the habits of these wild animals and how best to set the trap. I made a makeshift dog harness out of scraps of leather left over from Grandfather's earlier tanning days, when they made leather from their own cowhides.

My grandfather watched but never offered to help, just asking if what I was doing was necessary. In his view, in the north, the only reason you did anything was to maintain life, put food on the table, create a shelter and purchase the necessary clothing; any other work was wasteful. Grandfather did emphasize I should attend school and learn all I could. "No one can take away your education," he said.

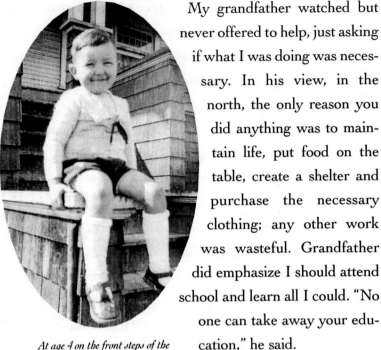

*At age 4 on the front steps of the Port Coquitlam farmhouse. Farm life was endlessly interesting but a bit lonely for a small boy.*

The harness now completed, the dog was hooked up to the sleigh. I persuaded Norman, an older boy who lived across the lake, to bring his two sleigh dogs over and harness all three together. He took one look at my makeshift harness and declared it too weak. "It will break," he predicted.

I persuaded him to try it and all three dogs were harnessed without any trouble. Norman gave them the mush signal in French and off we went, trotting behind. It was a nice sight. Then I got the idea I should ride on the sleigh. My section of harness snapped and off went the three dogs into a deep snow bank, barking and howling. To make it worse, Norman's second dog was blind, and this added to its panic. Norman had to go into the snow bank and unravel the dogs. I felt cut down to size, no more city show-off stuff.

I had chores to do: milk one cow, help with the milk separator, bring in wood and work around the barn. I really enjoyed working with my grandfather. He could not read or write but shared his knowledge with me and taught me without my knowing it: how to be observant, remember what you saw, keep a picture image of everything in your mind. He made many things on the farm and showed me how to use the tools he had brought from Quebec. He was a craftsman, as so many French-Canadians were.

## *And Back Again*

Come spring, a telegram arrived from Vancouver requesting my mother return to the Blackburn Market and she left at once by train. Her business partner came by train to drive the pick-up back to Vancouver. In April, I left Duclos School part-way through grade six, and off we went in the truck to Vancouver, taking along my Aunt Rose, now 18.

It was a slippery trip on the muddy farm roads. We were pulled out of the ditch by horses many times, eventually arriving on paved roads. We reached Spokane, Washington, at 2 a.m. Out on the road at 6 a.m. the next day; we arrived in Vancouver at midnight exhausted. I was excited to be back in the city but apprehensive about what lay ahead in school.

My mother had rented a nice house for $25 per month near Hastings School where I had left grade six the previous October. It was now late April and I resumed my schooling. The teachers found me far behind in my studies, and expressed doubts that I would pass.

I could not catch up, but I had not lost my skills as a trader. I would bring one of my Indian-made goods to school, show it to the teacher who passed it around for all to see. Later on, I would be approached on the school grounds by one of the kids who wanted the beaded item and a trade was made. It was not long before I had traded all my stuff and got back such treasures as parts of a bicycle – lamp, reflectors and air pump.

The school marks were posted at the end of the school year, with my name last. I was sorry to fail but somehow I felt more advanced than my classmates.

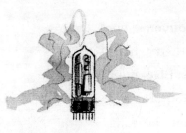

# Chapter Two
# Teen Years

My teenage years set the pattern of my life. Before age 12, I had been shipped off twice to my grandparents' care in northern Alberta. Each time it cost a grade in school. I don't believe I was a slow learner; it was the different grade standards between provinces, the upheaval of moving, and the language change. Back home in Vancouver, the teachers made no effort to upgrade me but simply commented, "We have a big one here."

I was more worldly than my classmates, having traveled to Alberta by train and car. Motoring through the Okanagan, we came upon truckloads of freshly picked apples on their way to the dump while people suffering through the Depression couldn't afford to buy them. Some apples rolled off the trucks, and these we gladly consumed, saving some for the prairie grandparents. It was hard to believe – people were hungry and farmers were paid to dump their produce.

In Vancouver, my mother worked hard managing her Blackburn Market chicken and egg stall. She put in long hours, six days a week. Her work didn't end until late most evenings. Being her only child, I had what attention time permitted, but I was expected to do my share in the house and the business.

*Alma Potvin in front of the Hastings Street house in 1938. Mother was known for her ability to make pennies go a very long way.*

Candling eggs in the basement was part of my share. Eggs were placed two or three in one hand, in front of a lamp covered so that only a ray of light shone on the eggs. The defective eggs showed blood spots inside. Those not too far gone were saved for the bakeries. Double yolks were segregated for special sale. Every cent was sought diligently. My eyes were often sore and red for next day's school.

There was no refrigeration those days, just ice blocks

delivered cold and dripping. Chickens were brought home before becoming too old to sell, and my job was to wash and scrub the chicken feet. These were boiled for broth. The chickens were boiled too and made into chicken jelly that was placed in small containers, which sold for 10¢ each – a real delicacy and a good seller.

Mother saved her money carefully and every now and then would buy something nice. A mantel clock with chimes, $15, three easy monthly payments of $5 each at Shores Jewelers on Hastings Street in Vancouver. I still have the clock and cherish it.

## Hard Work and a New Car

We had a new car, a 1937 Ford coupe that sat in the garage for Sundays when time permitted trips to Langley Prairie and Mission to visit relatives. It was the Great Depression. Yes, my mother worked hard, but that was the norm of the day. Some not so fortunate resented her accomplishments, but among the relatives, she was looked up to.

The radio bug bit me at age 14. I started tinkering with radios after school and long into the night, attempting to receive the most distant stations. We had moved to East Hastings Street, North Burnaby, the present site of the Dolphin Theatre. My grandparents came out to stay with us for a year. My frugal grandfather Napoleon could not understand my interest in radio as he could see no tangible results and often asked why I was wasting so much time. Accustomed to turning down the wick on the coal oil lamp in the prairies to save on kerosene, it seemed to him a waste of electricity to use a 10-watt, clear light bulb. He frequently turned it off as I worked, feeling I had used enough power.

Just the same, grandfather and I often went for walks together. While he was illiterate, never having gone to school, and spoke only French, I learned a lot translating what we saw, read or experienced. Much useful philosophy was passed on, creating thought patterns beyond my years.

My grandparents returned to the prairies, dismantling their farm and moving their log house into the village of Bonnyville, Alberta. Without Grandfather Napoleon I found myself alone and learned how to take care of myself.

*My mother's chicken stall in Blackburn's Market which was a regular farmers' market located at the corner of Robson and Seymour streets in Vancouver. In photo (left to right) are: Aunt Rosa Marcoux, Fred Pyle, mother's business partner, and my mother Alma Potvin.*

School progressed well in most subjects. I excelled at what we called electricity, woodworking, sheet metal, science, Canadian history and spelling. I did not do well in British History or English Literature. The fierce teachers of these subjects and the vice principal had me terrified, freezing my learning processes. The vice principal had been a major in the British Army in the First World War.

If we didn't address him as Major, his considerable wrath spilled over. Upon reaching grade eight at 15 years old, I had the bad luck to have the Major as my homeroom teacher. The story was that a war injury had left the Major with a metal plate in his head. At times while lecturing, he would drift off, stare, and in a few minutes, resume teaching again. Lord help the student caught clowning when he came to. I was very nervous in his class; his approach to learning was to threaten and belittle the students.

In my third week of grade eight, fumbling away at memorizing the "Lady of the Lake," I had enough, left and never returned to school. Besides, my physical size and my interests were very much out of sync with my classmates.

### A Job I Could Do

My mother was devastated, as she had hoped for an educated son. I was promptly informed I would have to find work. "Not to worry, Mother," I said, "I have found a job at the local radio repair shop at $3.50 per week." It is true that the pay was $3.50 a week, but only when Joe could afford it. My boss, Joe Nickerson, had been an active radio ham, VE5 AO, before wartime regulations closed down all radio amateurs in Canada.

41

It was 1939, war had been declared, and many radio people joined the services, skills in radio communications being in demand by the military. I was left to attend the public address systems my employer rented out to the sideshows at the Vancouver Pacific National Exhibition. The Vancouver audio king and ham operator Cyril Trott was also in the P.A. business and was our main competitor.

I made sure all P.A. systems were working and played records for the "girlie show" when it was not closed down by the city police. I was taken for much older, well, 21 anyway, so was accepted into the group. Sharing the back of the tent with the dancing girls was pretty educational for a 15-year-old. Some of the girls who had taken time off from their sales clerk jobs with Woodward's department store to get a little extra income worried about being recognized by old customers. But who would expect them in the girlie show on the midway?

When the shows moved to Victoria, my boss sent me off with all the P.A. equipment to set up, operate and collect fees from the show operators. I didn't know it was necessary to reserve sleeping accommodation on the night boat to Victoria and spent all night on the deck with the carnies who swigged away at mickeys of rye.

I set up the equipment, operated the record player and rolled up in canvas to sleep on the makeshift stage. Collection day was a problem, some of the showmen paying freely, others trying to slip away without paying the youngster. Finally I collected – it was all coins so it made a very heavy bundle.

The madam of the girlie show offered to look after the money bag for me. She had taken a motherly interest in me during the week so I felt comfortable with the offer.

When my work was done, I came back to retrieve my money bag. Nothing and no one was to be found but the wooden makeshift stage. The madam's husband was known as a promoter and looked like Colonel Sanders. My boss later tracked him down in Vancouver, but "Colonel Sanders" claimed he hadn't been able to find me at the fair. Of course he didn't have the money right then, but promised repayment. He finally did return the bag, but in a considerably lighter state.

As has happened so often in my life with people I met, I saw Colonel Sanders 10 years later in Prince Rupert where I was demonstrating two-way radio to '99 Cabs.' The sale depended on Pop the pool hall owner and operator to check the performance of this new invention. Into the cab came Pop, a.k.a. Colonel Sanders, looking older, but I recognized him right away. Not a word was exchanged at first about the missing money. Pop bought the radio system, cash in advance. He finally said, "Say, I remember you. Boy, did we have a hard time finding your boss to return your money bag."

My mother's partner in the poultry stall at Blackburn's Market was Mr. Fred Pyle who took an interest in me and my work with radios. His sideline was wheeling and dealing in used cars. Now I was 16, he thought I should have a car, and I soon had, for $75, a 1928 Coupe twin-ignition Nash, with wire spoke wheels and white sidewall tires, plus a debt to Mr. Pyle.

## *A Business of My Own*

I talked my mother into funding a radio course at Sprott Shaw Radio School in Vancouver. The course lasted only a few months but brought me into contact with what was going on in the world. This training qualified me for my own part-time radio repair business operated out of our North Burnaby home. I called it Potvin Radio Service and promoted it through advertisements in the Glenburn News and a billboard I painted myself.

The air force was recruiting students right out of radio school and shipping them off to England. The Merchant Marine was taking wireless operators as soon as they learned radio telegraphy. I was still too young to join any service but could see what was in the future.

I found a job at a Vancouver radio repair shop, tending the store and repairing the radios and small appliances that came our way. I soon learned another lesson in marketing. It was the fad of the day to have your radio tubes tested. This involved placing each individual tube in the tester, adjusting the settings and looking for good, normal or weak readings. It was possible to adjust the settings to make a weak tube read good or a good tube read weak.

When I was testing tubes for a customer, the boss, with his charming manner, would ask me to attend to something else as he called in the customer to observe the meter readings. When a good tube

*At age 16 I opened my first business and hung out my hand-made sign. I serviced domestic radios in the neighborhood. For problems beyond my skill I turned to more experienced repairmen increasing my knowledge with each consultation.*

was made to read weak, it was ceremoniously tossed in the paper-filled waste basket and a new tube sold in its place.

After the customer had left, pleased with the boss' attention, the old tube was retrieved and placed in the new just-discarded carton. Popular Mechanics magazine of the day ran an article called, "The Radio Man Will Gyp You if You Don't Look Out." It was indeed very true and a prevalent practice at the time. I soon learned these marketing tactics but tried to avoid them.

Other workers had left to join the air force. One day, delighted to hear from an ex-worker now overseas, my boss read me the letter, which expressed regrets at having skimmed cash and promised to make it up after the war. We were not doing much business and my boss warned me I would regret it if I skimmed any money.

I was not sensitive enough to be modest and boasted about how well I was doing in my own part-time radio repair business in the evenings and on weekends. It wasn't long before I was sent packing with the inference I was redirecting store clients to my own evening business. I insisted this was not the case, but my big mouth had gotten me into a lot of trouble. What a lesson this was, and I was getting it free!

## The Air Force Called

I felt strongly the lack of contact with my own age group and I knew I was headed for military service. The Royal Canadian Air Force, a volunteer service, was my choice. An ex-wing commander from World War I, acting on his own, ran an air cadet movement in Vancouver. This was not sanctioned by the air force but no doubt looked upon with favour. World War I high-collared uniforms were made available to the cadets. These were piled in a storeroom at the ex-commander's Hudson Terraplane automobile dealership on Burrard Street in Vancouver.

I befriended a cadet who gave me the lowdown, explaining that the cadets came from more privileged Point Grey families and the wing commander selected the applicants himself. The cadets gathered Friday evenings at the old Stanley Park armoury, long since demolished. My friend

*My Air Force Cadet pre-World War II uniform.*

paraded me in to see the wing commander, who was standing uniformed and medalled, enjoying the diversion from his car sales operation. With him was another man sporting a warrant officer's uniform. I believe he was with the regular force and was there to support this maverick cadet movement and presumably to direct cadets into applying as air crew for the regular service.

I was introduced and it was soon established that I was a school dropout, but my friend pointed out I was a radio repair man and had trained at Sprott Shaw Radio School. The wing commander, about to say no, looked at the warrant officer who said, "Wireless Air Gunner," and I was told to pick up my uniform. Was I ever pleased with myself!

I enjoyed the feeling of belonging with the other cadets and was happy when asked to teach a small group about the workings of radio. I was proud when told to wear on my sleeve the sparks emblem depicting a radio man, and the

*4559 East Hastings Street in Burnaby, mother's home from 1938 to 1948. All the relatives and friends from Bonnyville stayed here when visiting the big city. The Dolphin Theatre now sits on the old house site.*

propeller indicating a "Leading Aircraftsman." We drilled, we marched, we had target practice, we had aircraft identification, all of it whetting the appetite of young fellows for the adventure ahead.

To tide me over until I could enlist, I found a job in a golf club manufacturing plant at $7.50 per week. I ran the drill press inserting lead pellets into the wooden clubs to bring them up to weight, then inserted the cover plate. It was an exacting job that I did well, and my pay was bumped up to $12.50 per week.

After work on Saturday mornings, I would change into my uniform, buttons polished and shoes shined. We wore steel cleats on our heels, which made an impressive clicking sound as we walked. Getting off the streetcar at Robson and

Richards streets, I would head for my mother's chicken stall at Blackburn Market and stand around talking. Cadets were often taken for enlisted men and as such admired.

On parade one Friday night at the Armouries, we waited, standing for more than an hour, for the arrival of Billy Bishop, the World War II air ace. The war hero asked where I earned my sparks. We cadets were in awe and I guess this was the effect he was meant to create.

The air force operated WETP, a wireless training program being taught at Vancouver Technical School. At age 17, I was pre-enlisted in the air force and allowed to attend classes, living at home as a civilian but receiving air force pay. The instructors knew their business and it wasn't long before we had absorbed a heavy dose of technical smarts and were proficient in radio telegraphy.

Exhilarated and a bit apprehensive, I was sworn into His Majesty's Service at age 18. Our group was destined for Montreal to be uniformed and indoctrinated in the way of the service.

# CHAPTER 3
# AIR FORCE

I had made it. I was in the air force, signed up and on my way to Montreal to learn how to be an airman. I felt the thrill of belonging, no longer a dropout but a part of the regular flow of society. And I was going to the soul city of my French-Canadian family.

Our destination was the Montreal No. 1 Wireless School where wireless operators and radio mechanics were trained for overseas and cross-country postings. Basic training came first so we were trundled off to Lachine to be kept on the run for six weeks in the freezing weather. A good part of that time spent was scrubbing floors and cleaning windows that were still wet from the efforts of the crew directly ahead of us.

There were some shocks in store for naive young airmen at Montreal Wireless School. We got frequent lectures on venereal disease and saw colour movies showing advanced gonorrhea, with the poor victim's testicles swollen to the size of cantaloupes.

Then came the exercise of detecting the disease – the so-called short arm inspection. Some 60 of us were marched into the gym, told to drop our pants and underwear and to cup our genitals so the Doc could get a quick look for drips as he passed by.

A corporal guard was posted at the door to keep out the curious, but along came three airwomen wanting to use the gym.

"Dey can't come into dis place," shouted the doc in his Quebec English, but they had already pushed past the guard and got an unexpected mass demonstration of the male anatomy times 60.

They screamed and ran out in shock.

Our Vancouver wireless group was kept together with a few additions from Newfoundland and the Bahamas. For three months we were retaught, but at a lower level, all the stuff we had learned at the WETP in Vancouver.

The WETP director, Ken Wheeler, also a radio ham, excelled at pushing his students to the limit. Ken, hearing I had been to Sprott Shaw Radio School, asked that I not be a smart ass in class. He needn't have bothered; the lessons in math and chemistry were way over my head. It was only with special help that I graduated.

In the WETP radio telegraphy class, our instructor, a

retired CPR telegrapher who had been an operator during the rum-running days on the coast, sought perfection. Many of us came quite close; I was one of the top two operators in the class. I practiced with my homemade short-wave receiver, copying five-letter cypher from some unknown military source.

The next stage of training in Montreal, the Wireless Electrical Radio Mechanics course, wasn't so easy, because of my poor education and my devotion to a beautiful airwoman. But once again, I scraped through and was slated with a few others for a further six weeks of training in VHF (very high frequency) radio, a new type of radio, which had played an important part in the Battle of Britain.

Frequently, the recruiting officer visited class attempting to entice us to transfer as wireless air gunners, for which promotion was assured. Some did transfer, were trained in gunnery, shipped overseas and were reported missing while we were still completing our studies.

## A Whole New World

My first venture into Montreal was like entering a new world. I spoke enough French to get by but in uniform I was pegged as English until I spoke. Then the warmth came forth. In one store the young clerk shouted, "Come out, Maman, come here, he speaks French just like us and he comes from Vancouver."

It was January and cold. I walked along the snowy streets lined by unfamiliar buildings but I felt at home. This was the city my grandparents had talked about so often on the farm in Bonnyville.

In my free time I explored the city. A couple of my classmates were ex-high school teachers who looked down on anyone speaking French with the locals. I kept my tongue to myself and accompanied them to the art centre and places of culture.

Other times, I made the rounds with an Acadian airman from New Brunswick. But a problem came up when my Acadian friend stopped by the Catholic church and I had to hang around until he came out. Soon the Catholic padre at the wireless school called me in for a talk. "Well, mon garçon, why are you not attending mass and confession?" he asked. I explained I was Protestant. "That you cannot be, you speak French and have a French name." I informed him of my radical breakaway community and that I had been baptized in the United Church. "Too bad, a pity," he said, "Carry on."

The culture had a strong pull for me. I was comfortable with the Quebecers, finding I could express feelings I found difficult to express in English. However, back in the Wireless School, I felt the same pull speaking English with my classmates. I guess I was a hybrid – an asset I realized in the business world after the war.

*Montreal #1 Wireless School on Parade in 1942. Some of us were assigned to a precision squad practicing until we were letter perfect. I enjoyed the discipline of the manoeuvres.*

During my first months in the service, the American Ambassador to Canada died suddenly. Ottawa requested the Wireless School in Montreal to send an honour guard for the ceremony. After five days of intensive training and more training, 30 of us were left to form an elite precision squad, able to march complex drill patterns by numbers which we recited to ourselves. One wrong turn or step and the whole presentation was out of whack.

White webbing, rifles, and bayonets were handed out and away we went to Ottawa. As often happens, little planning went into the ceremony itself. On the railway platform we were jammed in against the army and navy units, so crowded there was no space to display our skill.

When the Ambassador's coffin was lifted into the baggage car and the command "Present Arms" was given, the soldier in front of me sliced open his ear with his bayonet!

55

Blood ran down his neck to his collar and uniform. No one moved as we were taught to carry on and disregard such things. Even a collapsed comrade was to be walked over.

It was my only precision squad appearance, but it was strangely satisfying to summon the inner discipline necessary to perform the drills. So it was in the air force on this side of the ocean.

## Another Change of Plan

When I joined the air force, getting married wasn't in my plans. I had never once thought of marriage. Even dating girls had a much lower priority than my goal of gaining an education in radio technology. But then, what do you do when you fall in love? My theory has always been when you have the right answer, don't dilly-dally wasting time, act on it. Jean and I were married shortly before my 19th birthday, the first air force couple to wed.

Jean, a Scottish-born Montrealer, was an airwoman wireless operator in training at the school. My Acadian friend had looked into her dark eyes and pronounced her loyal and true. Permission for the wedding was required. The Commanding Officer had me wire my mother for approval, not before advising me that I didn't have to get married as "the service could work things out."

"Oh, no, sir," I answered, "this is the real thing," saluted and marched out.

Jean, one of the top students in her class, graduated a

corporal. Lots of fun was poked at me for being a mere air-man with a corporal wife.

And so it went, until one day Sergeant Schwartz burst into the barrack room where I was lying on my top bunk contemplating some radio circuit.

"Potvin," he shouted, "how would you like to be posted to the West Coast?" He told me that "Ma," as we knew the women's division administrator, had asked Jean if she would like to be posted there. The few overseas postings were filled and the rest of us were to be dispersed across the country. Of course we both wanted to go west, but the sergeant reminded me that postings went to names drawn out of a hat.

So a drawing was arranged, and the three wireless class-es were assembled to watch. Sgt. Schwartz handed the name slips to the officer in charge, and as the routine went on, I noticed his little finger was curled up into his fist, and out came the name Potvin. Jean's name was drawn as well.

I can't say exactly how this happened but I had an inkling, and I believe the service had a heart after all. I think Ma and the drill sergeant wanted to give the first couple married in the air force a chance.

And I remembered my mother and the veil over my head.

Our training completed, Jean and I were posted to Vancouver; Western Air Command and Jericho Beach Repair Depot where Stranraer amphibian patrol craft were based. Immediately I was placed on a VHF work crew to fit aircraft and control towers with the new VHF equipment. The West Coast was gearing up for a more intense Pacific war. Jean was a wireless operator on the weather-gathering station that communicated with Air Force coastal locations several times a day.

To add to our good fortune, we were able to live at home, although I was away much of the time on assignments up and down the coast. Our work included fitting VHF equipment into Mitchell bombers at Boundary Bay. The summer weather was unusually hot and working on these bombers parked on the sun-baked tarmac was no cool job. Our only concession to heat was to discard all clothing except coveralls.

At Sea Island, now Vancouver International Airport, we equipped a squadron of Kittyhawk fighter planes. The installation involved crawling inside the fuselage through a small access panel on the side of the aircraft. It took a while to reach a comfortable position lying on your back with pulleys and cables poking into your sides. Tools were handed in through the panel and placed on my chest. I could then do my work somewhat akin to a sea otter feeding on clams – not a job for anyone with claustrophobic tendencies. I couldn't possibly do it today, besides the side panel of a 747 would be a better fit for me now!

Soon we were sent off to Tofino on the west coast of Vancouver Island to fit up a squadron of Hurricane fighters. The Tofino airport was, in those days, protected by gun emplacements manned by the army. Nearby Long Beach, about the only sandy beach on the west coast of the island, was studded with rusty, vertical steel rails, driven into the sand to impede possible landings by the Japanese.

This was before the A-bombs at Hiroshima and Nagasaki. The Japanese were still perceived as a threat to the West Coast, although they were being rolled back in the South Pacific.

Japan had made air raids on Dutch Harbour in Alaska, and Estevan Lighthouse near us was shelled one evening, apparently by a Japanese submarine, although there was later speculation it could have been hit by accident during Navy gunnery practice. Japanese balloons with an explosive basket hanging below were being launched in the jet stream from Japan and many found their way into the interior woodlands of B.C.

The conditions at Tofino were primitive compared to other bases. We worked outdoors in the constant West Coast rain. The barrack buildings were mired in muck. Planks placed in the mud as walkways floated around the entrance way. No beds, we slept on the floor. The airmen stationed at Tofino had not seen the "outside" for some

*At Tofino, B.C. on the west coast of Vancouver Island*
*we fitted Hurricane fighters like this with the VHF AM radio equipment.*

months and were feeling restless for outside contact, prefer-
ably of the female persuasion. Someone suggested a dance
and this mushroomed into a memorable event.

Our partners – they were termed hostesses – were
brought from Port Alberni, down the Alberni Canal and
across the mouth of Barkley Sound in the hold of an old fish
packer, then trucked from Ucluelet to the base over a primitive gravel road. Just like other base supplies.

Since the air was anything but sweet in the hold, and the
boat rolled wildly when it hit the open swells, most of our
hostesses were the worse for wear when they arrived, but
were soon raring to go to the party.

Anticipation at the base was running high. The dance was
on and the airmen were all sprucing up for the big event. But
those of us on temporary duty there were outsiders. We were
not on the station strength and knew nobody except those we
worked with.

Maybe it was just as well.

As the evening advanced, the gathering grew rowdier.

60

The Catholic and Anglican padres who gave approval to the importation of the ladies were looking on with dismay, conferring frequently as the level of excitement escalated. In time, we ignorant outsiders realized liquor was being dispensed out in the trees. The place was really jumping (I suddenly knew what the phrase meant). Before long the padres had exceeded their toleration point and called for closure.

The dance ended but the socially starved airmen were not to be stopped. The girls were accommodated in one of the bunk houses and partying continued until the service police were called in. We temporary workers kept our distance to avoid any chance of being arrested, and maybe kept on the base. Early in the morning, the women were hurried away for the trip home. The only signs of revelry remaining were women's underclothes hanging in the trees around the barrack block!

The men figured it was a huge joke, but the station commander didn't agree and banned dances and hostesses at the Tofino base for the duration.

*Airmen and Friends*

Back at Jericho Beach, my working base, only a few of us had bench radio repair and diagnostic experience, so civilian technicians were engaged in order to keep up with the volume of repair work sent in by the various squadrons. There was a big backlog of work. The question was: "Where was the bottleneck?"

We all had a pretty good idea. The supervising office had some 17 staff from squadron leader down to sergeant. The repair section had three civilian and 10 service radio technicians. This was bureaucracy at its best, work directives appeared daily on the notice board without any one of the 17 ordering replacement parts.

One day my name appeared on the notice board to report for special military training. We were trained as replacements for raiding parties: to go ashore, silently overcome resistance and return with radar components which would determine the enemy's capabilities. I will not relate the unsavoury and necessary skills we were taught. We were run off our asses for three weeks, returned to normal duty and forgotten.

Friends that I made in the Force were of the short duration of a particular training period or temporary posting. After the war, forgetting rank, lasting friendships were generated. Many of the technical types were drawn together by our enthusiasm to get back on the air with our Radio Amateur Licence. Through amateur radio – which came to be known as ham radio – we met again. Two great friends I remember well are Archie Mitchell, ex-flight lieutenant (radar), and Marvin Wilson, warrant officer, Aero Engine section. Flight Lt. Mitchell was in charge of radar stores, an off-limits area because of radar secrecy, located on the far side of our hangar.

Before the war, Archie and his wife operated a hotel in Luskar, Alberta. He was keen on radio and wanted to become a ham radio operator. In those days, it was difficult traveling in Alberta. So the radio inspector of the day, believing in Archie's proficiency, issued him a licence by mail, subject to passing an examination sometime later in Edmonton.

But the war intervened, and without examination the inspector recommended Archie to the Air Force, then desperate for radio people and their knowledge.

With such an introduction, Archie, an older man, was accepted and given a commission. The Force soon found it had an officer who did not have the technical know-how to do his job.

The answer was simple: promote him. He became Flight Lieutenant Archie Mitchell appointed as radar stores officer. This isolated him and provided a senior role model for young airmen. The job required a minimum of technical smarts and was just right for Archie. Archie himself passed this story on to me with his Scottish brogue and deep chuckle.

After the war, I constructed a mobile radio unit for Marv Wilson's car, with one channel for talk within B.C. and a second channel for contact with international stations. Marv was one of the founding partners of Auto Marine Electric which became a sizeable firm in B.C. Marv, enthralled with his mobile equipment, spent hours in the company parking lot talking to radio hams, while his partner, not sharing his enthusiasm, worked hard inside.

Marv's bank manager friend, Bob Dunn, also a ham, arranged for Marv's share of the loan to finance the start of Auto Marine Electric. They remained friends and when they retired, joined in the business of radio surplus, taking over the "Ham Shack" in Vancouver. Marv was overly generous by nature, especially with ham friends; Bob, the ex-bank manager, was naturally prudent. A visit to the Ham Shack meant I left with pockets full of free goodies, while Bob and Marv argued heatedly over a few sales tax pennies that had gone astray.

I have the fondest memories of my air force buddies and their friendship towards me, a younger, unworldly fellow when I was in the service.

## When Do You Salute?

Jericho wasn't without its characters.

Joe Philliponi was a corporal motor transport driver, a natural since in civvie life he was connected with Eagle Time Delivery, a motorcycle and sidecar delivery service. Eagle Time was speedy, low cost and made deliveries all over Vancouver, including bringing liquor to the thirsty.

Joe later ran the famous Penthouse, a late-night drinks and girls club in downtown Vancouver, until he was shot dead in his office, many years after his air force days.

On the base, if you were short of money, Joe's former

delivery office would lend you ten bucks in exchange for your unused liquor ration. Joe was a businessman and humanitarian – a combination you don't always see. We all spoke well of him.

He had no problem with the military police at the gate and enjoyed more freedom than the rest of us. He did many favours for officers and other ranks alike. And he did not seek reward, at least not at the moment.

Once acting as ombudsmen for complaints to Group Captain Chapman, another airman and I were meeting with him and we were so nervous, we couldn't bring up anything for fear of reprisal. In the middle of the meeting, in wandered Joe Philliponi, hat on crooked, tunic buttons undone, looking untidy and unfazed by the presence of authority.

Not saluting, Joe just said, "Hello," and the Group Captain replied, "Hello, Joe." We were left wondering how Joe achieved his status.

When we were all civilians again, I had dealings with Joe and his company, installing two-way VHF radio in his family's Diamond Cabs and the Penthouse. We installed a remote control unit, fitted under the counter at the bar, to give direct contact between the taxi drivers and the cabaret barman, which in some way resulted in a discreet flow of beautiful women to the club. The cabaret was memorable, with life-sized pictures of well-known entertainers. Bing Crosby, Nat King Cole and the like. There was a glass viewing room covered with curtains, providing the management with an excellent view of the partyers. Some well-known government people were said to frequent the facility.

As the war seemed to be winding down, station discipline became more lax: fewer parades, make-work projects. The officers and NCOs were contemplating their futures and no longer showed much interest.

In August 1945, the A-bombs were dropped on Hiroshima and Nagasaki in Japan. We were stunned, but relieved that we would not now be sent to the Pacific Theatre.

## The Long Road Back

Then, out of the blue, I was told the Jericho Beach repair depot was closing down and I was transferred to Penhold, Alberta.

Penhold was in a state of disarray. They had no record of my posting. They had to write Western Air Command for my file, and meanwhile I was assigned to a work group in a hangar. It was a lesson in the waste of war. The job was to lay thousands of dollars worth of radio equipment out on the apron, so that a roller machine could flatten it out.

We were told the equipment had to be destroyed so it would be unusable on the market. However, an enterprising motor transport driver was trucking odds and ends out to Calgary for use by radio hams who had been shut down during the war years and couldn't wait to get back on the air.

When I asked if my records had arrived, the adjutant said no, and did I want a discharge? Just like that.

So off to Calgary I was sent to wait for my records at the former airdrome and repair depot some miles out of town.

Again, they had no idea at the station why we'd been sent there but gave us an advance on our pay.

We had to find bunks and settle in. The place was in confusion, but I had never been on a station where the food was so good. It was contracted out to a private company.

We lined up a hundred or more at meal times, and did our washing day after day, because there was a good laundry room and it was something to do. I also carried on with high school correspondence courses I had begun with the Department of Education in Victoria.

*The real world was looming ahead.*

It was interesting to see the differences in the attitudes of the airmen awaiting discharge. Some knew what they were going to do; others were apprehensive. Look at it this way: in the Force on the bases, if you needed new duds or shoes, you just asked. You could go on sick parade or make an appointment with the dentist. You could get a 48-hour pass every second or third week, even a 72-hour pass at times.

You became a kept person, institutionalized, and some were reluctant to give up a good thing, remembering the Hungry Thirties when jobs and money were scarce.

I kept checking at the orderly room for my papers. One day they arrived, and we went through the old drill of confirming that the records matched my person, but finally I got a travel voucher to Western Air Command for discharge. The discharge officer, who thanked me for my service to the Crown and discharged me, turned out to be a guy I had known as a corporal, and not a very good one at that.

I left the service with 30 days' severance pay and $100 for new civilian clothing.

It was great to be away from the Air Force, but I realized I had to get cracking on a real job, and all I wanted to do was work with radio.

When Jean and I were posted to Vancouver, we first lived at my mother's place, 4559 East Hastings in Burnaby, and travelled three hours a day to our jobs in the Air Force.

Jean's widowed mother, Janet Mount, soon followed us from Montreal to the Coast. We pooled our resources and started to look for a house to buy. Mrs. Mount thought the east end of Vancouver was uncouth, so together she and Jean found a house needing repair at 4754 Belmont Avenue, two blocks from the Jericho base and with an ocean view.

We bought the house in April 1944, and kept it until 1971, when daughter Heather completed university and married. By that time, Jean and I and our son Bruce had

*Montreal in May 1943. Jean and I were the first Air Force couple to marry.*
*We met and fell in love while in Communications Training at the #1 Wireless School.*
*Happily we were both later transferred to the West Coast.*

been living at Lillooet Lake for several years.

Grandparents Marcoux came from Alberta to visit us at Christmas in 1946. Grandfather Napoleon, my childhood mentor and the one I always wanted to please, seemed to resent my success in a life he didn't understand. Too much had changed and, most difficult of all, I had moved from a French-speaking environment where he was a valued guide to a totally Anglophone environment where his teachings were out of touch.

He returned to Bonnyville, but after some years moved back to the Coast to live with one of his sons in the French-Canadian community of Maillardville.

A couple of years after my discharge, my mother died, just before Heather was born. At age 39, my mother had succumbed to cancer after suffering unsuccessful experimental radium treatments. My father had died suddenly on Granville Street a few years earlier after dental surgery.

Looking back, I owe the air force a lot. Enlisting at 18 years of age, learning the military structure, getting technical training and meeting my first wife Jean set me on a positive path in life. While I was not sent to serve in any war zone, the air force could have had me serve anywhere in the world. Upon discharge, the re-establishment funds and low-interest loans made it possible to purchase land and build. It was this assistance that made it possible for us to build at Lillooet Lake. I had served my country; in turn Canada treated me well, for which I am grateful. Grandfather Napoleon would say: "You got too much you."

# CHAPTER 4
# FLYING RADIO MAN

When I hung up the blue serge uniform of the air force to become a civilian again, I gravitated to the life of a radio technician and found myself flying up the coast, and sometimes in the same old flying boats.

The Stranraers had gotten their discharge too, and our associate company, Queen Charlotte Airlines, bought them as war surplus.

It was an exciting and adventurous life, and I realize now that we shrugged off danger with the confidence of "it-won't-happen-to-me" youth.

There was a sense of satisfaction in doing a difficult job and there were some laughs as well as the heartbreak of losing companions to the implacable whim of nature.

I remember the black humour of the old saying, "If man were meant to fly he'd have wings."

Dixon Entrance

Queen Charlotte Islands

Prince Rupert

Whitesail Lake

Queen Charlotte City

Kemano

Hecate Strait

Butedale

Bella Bella

Pacific Ocean

Namu

Queen Charlotte Sound

Belize Inlet

Coal Harbour

Sullivan Bay

Alert Bay

Minstrel Island

Vancouver Island

Georgia Strait

Nootka

Powell River

Ucluelet

Stillwater

Port Alberni

Vancouver

Juan de Fuca Strait

I was abandoned on a mountainside unaware that my Strannie had crashed after leaving me.

I flew to the Queen Charlotte Islands in a balky, under-powered Cessna. We landed after the engine died and I had to climb out on a float to paddle it down the channel.

I went all the way to Ecuador with the Ansons that Queen Charlotte Airlines sold to an airline there. It was the first of several trips I made to South America to sell radio communications equipment.

It was an exciting life I found myself in after the war. I got into it because a friend who was working for Spilsbury and Hepburn, then a small company making radiotele-phones at the foot of Cardero Street in Vancouver, thought they could use another technician, and they took me on.

There were seven people working there when I started, but the company expanded quickly, became Spilsbury & Tindall and I finally set up my own company to deal with export sales.

## The Wild Blue Yonder

One of the B.C. trips called for a radiotelephone installa-tion for a diamond drilling crew at Whitesail Lake in the Tweedsmuir Park area. The radio telephone was crated, the 32-volt bank of batteries readied, the gas generator ordered and everything delivered to the QCA terminal. Off I went on the Stranraer with the equipment for Whitesail Lake on a Vancouver-to-Prince Rupert flight.

In the afternoon we spotted the sandy beach and log cabin at the end of the lake where we were to rendezvous. We circled, landed and taxied the aircraft hull up onto the beach. We unloaded in the proverbial middle of nowhere, sun shining on the high snow-topped mountains surrounding us.

"I'm going now," said the pilot after we got the equipment out of the plane. "I hope you'll be okay." They were the last words I'd ever hear him speak, but I didn't know that as I sat on a crate watching the flying boat leave the water, circle to gain altitude, then disappear between the high mountain peaks. A beautiful sight I'll never forget.

After a while, out of the woods came the native guide with five packhorses. Some of the horses had worn hides, exposing pink flesh which the packer treated with salve and covered with cloth before placing the pack saddle on top. A lead acid battery was tied on each side of the saddle, low down in case of spillage. The horses were cranky and the guide and I walked the trail with them, arriving in the dark of night at the bare-bones tent camp. The cook warmed up the stew, which included chunks of that morning's pancakes.

I was told a horse was shot when its hide became too worn. In any case all horses were shot in the late fall. In the spring, new horses were brought in from Burns Lake by road, trail and makeshift raft. It was a tough life for horses.

I completed the radiotelephone installation, stringing the

long wire antenna down a canyon and fastening it to large boulders, as there were no trees. And, as often happens, there was something missing from the order. The supplier had failed to ship the fuel tank for the generator. The only container available was the cook's wash basin so we punched a drain hole in the bottom, installed the gas line and sealed the joint with chewing gum.

We filled the wash-pan with gas, cranked up and made our phone calls to test the installation. Then we shut down and poured the surplus gas back into the gas container. Of course, dishes washed in the basin afterward had a whiff of petroleum, something pointed out loudly by the drilling crew.

When I phoned the shop Jack Tindall, who had joined the firm as third partner, said there would be a delay, and to stay put and wait for a new pick-up time. Some days later, the geologist and I hiked down the trail at dawn, an exhilarating experience amongst the towering glacial peaks with marmots aplenty for company. We waited at the lakeshore where we could be seen from the air and finally a Stranraer flying boat circled and landed.

I asked about the other Stranraer and its crew, and was shocked at the answer: "Didn't you hear? They crashed into the sea."

I listened in growing horror to the story. The old boat had gone on a mercy flight from Prince Rupert to the Queen Charlotte Islands to pick up a mother and child. It was evening, just enough time to make the return flight if there were no delays. Some local people were aboard, having been invited along for the trip.

But they were late getting away from Queen Charlotte City, and on the return flight, they found Prince Rupert socked in with ground fog. A warship in port was alerted to the circling aircraft and switched on its flood-lamps, but to no avail. It became dark, and although there was no ground-to-air communication, there was a radio navigation range, which the aircraft followed out to sea to try a landing.

This probably would have worked, but the hull skimmed a reef. The passengers and flight engineer were catapulted out as the bottom of the plane ripped open. Airborne again, the plane apparently flew on some distance before it nosed down and sank. Everyone aboard was lost.

Radio communications would have prevented this accident. It was only then that the Department of Transport took up the application by QCA for an aviation frequency. Even the use of the fishermen's frequency, 1630 khz, would have provided contact with fishermen on the water. But no air-to-boat communication was permitted. We had tried it unofficially before, and been ordered to desist.

It was a somber flight as we returned to Vancouver and the front page headlines. It was only by chance that I wasn't on that other flight.

Another memorable trip was flying to the Queen Charlotte Islands with my boss Jim Spilsbury in a small Cessna in not-too-good repair.

One summer day I was at the B.C. Packers Cannery at Namu installing new radio equipment. A call came from Jim. He had received his pilot's licence and was flying up-coast to Oscar Johnson's Belize Inlet camp. I was to stay put and he would pick me up later that day. What plans he had I didn't know and I don't think he did either. Jim just wanted to try his wings.

I plugged in a QCA crystal so I could pick up the new QCA frequency. Jim reported landing at Belize Inlet so I knew he should be along later in the day. Next came a call from Jim suggesting I proceed to Prince Rupert where he would meet me. Apparently there had been some aircraft trouble. I boarded the Union Steamships boat for Prince Rupert; a light plane passed by us as we steamed along, and I concluded it must be Jim.

But I was wrong. Later, at Prince Rupert, I heard the story of Jim's Belize Inlet landing. The water was glassy, a difficult landing situation, and the aircraft hit the water too soon. So Jim climbed a little, then let down again. But as he coasted in he struck a slick boom-stick, which pried the aircraft out of the water and onto the log float that housed the camp fuel supply. At first Jim thought he had made a safe landing, and announced his arrival on the radio, which was the transmission I heard in Namu.

Jim reported later he was shaking when he stepped out and found himself on the gas float, the propeller only inches from the gas tanks. Two QCA mechanics flew up to Belize Inlet with a rented Cessna replacement. They hammered out what needed straightening, patched the float with tar and flew the plane back to Vancouver. Jim carried on alone to Prince Rupert in the rented Cessna.

Together we installed the first QCA radio equipment at the Seal Cove seaplane base outside Prince Rupert. Now the northern portion of the airline operation was really in business. We had air-to-ground, as well as Vancouver-to-Rupert communication.

The Stranraer flying boat service to the Queen Charlotte Islands had been replaced with land-based aircraft, the Ansons, nicely refurbished for passenger service. The flight left Vancouver, refueled at Port Hardy and ended at Sandspit, on Moresby Island, the southerly one of the Queen Charlotte Islands. From there, passengers were bused to Alliford Bay to connect with another QCA float-plane service from Prince Rupert that serviced both Moresby and Graham Island.

Jim was anxious to see this service in operation and decided on the spur of the moment that we should fly to the Charlottes. "You have been to all the camps, perhaps you can drum up some further radio business," he said.

The next morning we taxied out with our baggage and repair tools. All morning we tried to get off the water, ending up several miles away in the mouth of the Skeena River.

The aircraft began to list, one float deep in the water. The right float had sprung a leak from the pressure of the repeated takeoff attempts. We taxied back to the QCA base at Seal Cove. The base pilot, Bill McLeod, thought the problem was the small prop on the Cessna. After the leak had been plugged with some gum material and all our baggage left behind to reduce weight, we attempted more takeoffs. Again, we couldn't get off the water.

"Maybe we will have to strip down to our shorts," Jim said. He thought it would make a great ad for the Cessna company. "West Coast radio men strip down to fly Cessna across Hecate Strait."

At that moment a seiner passed. Jim headed into the light swell from the boat and, boom boom, we were airborne and climbing. As we headed out in the sunset, 90 miles of sea to the Islands, Jim spoke in a reassuring tone although his message was hardly reassuring, "You know I just got my pilot's licence, so keep a lookout for boats below in case we go down."

Looking down, all I could see were large swells and frothy sea with the very occasional small dot of a vessel. The air force had taught me that in a sea like this, one either flipped on landing or was swallowed into the swells in a matter of minutes. I was resigned to my possible fate but hoped

79

I might be spared.

We tensed up more when the carburetor began icing. Down we would go, losing altitude rapidly. But after our downward plunge the ice would thaw and up we would climb again. We did the bunny-hop across Hecate Strait. That wasn't all. The controls had a backlash. They didn't respond immediately, and then overcorrected. Later, in Vancouver, an inspection revealed a frayed control cable.

But before nightfall, we reached Cumshewa Camp on Moresby Island. We joined the stampede of loggers to the mess hall when the dinner gong was sounded.

Next morning, Jim said he wasn't sure the aircraft would make it with both of us aboard and I should proceed to Queen Charlotte City alone. So I started off by going to Sandspit on a tug in seas so rough I had to belt myself down on the bunk in the wheelhouse. When we docked I got a ride to Alliford Bay, the seaplane base. To my delight, there was our cranky little Cessna tied to the float.

Jim and I decided to test our luck by flying to Masset at the upper end of Graham Island. A rough takeoff got us airborne and we headed up the east coast of the island. The skies grew darker and darker, and suddenly, at Dead Tree Point, we encountered a black wall of clouds. The only thing to do was circle back to Queen Charlotte City. The sea was churned up and we bounced, hitting a wave top, landing with the door swinging open on my side.

I had had just about enough of this trip, but after a good

night's sleep, we were both eager to go on now that we had clear skies.

This time I asked Jim to follow the old wooden plank road up Graham Island from Queen Charlotte City. We flew at a lower altitude and had no carburetor icing. But over Masset the engine quit. Everything became silent. Jim touched my knee and joked, "What you say we radio Vancouver and double our insurance?" No sooner said, the engine started up again and we gained altitude.

I suggested we ditch in shallow water in a tidal pond below us, but, encouraged with the engine running again, Jim took the Cessna out over Masset Inlet. Again the engine quit and we landed in the inlet. It was a rough landing., "You better get out on the float," Jim said, and after we drifted awhile in the current, we paddled in to the dock.

The Cessna was damaged and the engine was not working. We boarded the Queen Charlotte Airlines Norseman to Rupert, thankful for its size and sturdiness.

Jim got through by radiotelephone to the QCA office. Johnny Hatch, the chief pilot, was furious that Jim, an inexperienced pilot, had taken a rental aircraft of unknown pedigree over 90 miles of water to the Queen Charlottes. Not only that, he had not reported his flight plan. Johnny had reported us missing, believing we were still in the mid-coastal region.

Looking back, I can understand Jim wanting to do what his own pilots did and my readiness to be part of the action and build up the radio company. But our egos blinded us to rational thinking. We treated it as a joke, but we had been courting death. It just wasn't our time to go. The Cessna made the return trip to Vancouver on board one of the Union steamships.

## Unexpected Adventures

One of QCA's great pilots was Bill Peters. Bill could navigate through weather few others would attempt. He left QCA for a year to fly a Grumman Goose for British Guyana Airways in and out of Brazil, then returned to QCA.

He was one of the pilots to fly seven Ansons QCA sold to Aerovias Equitorianus of Ecuador, and I hitched rides with them as I made my way from Miami to Venezuela, Colombia and Ecuador, pursuing radio sales for Spilsbury & Tindall.

I well remember the 1953 dirt landing strip in Quito and the QCA air frame mechanic, called the woodworker, attempting to glue a plywood fitting to the tail section, only to be frustrated by the dusty wind gumming up his freshly glued patch. The Ansons, built from plywood as a twin-engine air force training plane, needed a lot of maintenance. The tail wheels kept falling off from landing on the rough strips.

A few years before, after my discharge from the air force in 1945, I had no thought such adventures lay ahead.

*The original Spilsbury & Hepburn Waco aircraft used for radio repair flights up and down the B.C. coast*

I had been working with Uncle Bill Marcoux, an accomplished craftsman, doing house renovations, manufacturing wooden wheelbarrows for Woodwards Department Store and hardwood cold air registers for heating companies.

A fellow radio ham, Jimmy Williamson, radio call VE5 ADV, got me a job at Spilsbury and Hepburn, a company formed during the war to meet the urgent need for civilian radiotelephones in isolated areas.

The partners, ham radio enthusiasts, had maintained contact over the air in prewar days; Jim Hepburn, VE5 HP in Victoria, and Jim Spilsbury, VE5 BR at Savary Island up the B.C. coast. Both were brilliant radio tinkerers but had limited business know-how.

Hep had been hand-making radio telephones out of

whatever parts were available in wartime. Spilsbury, operating from his boat, installed the units as fast as they could be made. Hepburn kept few diagrams of his work and left it to Spilsbury to improvise in the field.

I was elated to land the job. Most of the staff were busy installing "KAAR" marine radiotelephones in fishing vessels and I joined them. KAAR equipment was made in Palo Alto, California, and this spurred the company to make its own, much-improved line of marine radiophones.

The demand for faster transportation to the up-coast camps led to the company's purchase of a Waco airplane on floats. This took me and some of our technicians to many up-coast locations and the west coast of Vancouver Island.

The company's air service was so popular that QCA, Queen Charlotte Airlines, was born, headed by Jim Spilsbury. The radio company's aircraft became part of QCA.

## We Worked at It

I installed the various aircraft radios as they became available, although we did not have our own frequency or land-line interconnections for some time. Frequently I was at the QCA seaplane base at the Vancouver airport in the very early morning hours before takeoff time. Then I hurried to the shop at the foot of Cardero Street to put in my day's work. There was no overtime pay but I was excited at being part of a growing endeavour.

To really be part of the team we were expected to work very long hours and purchase shares in the company, as I did.

Satisfying our isolated customers was a taxing job. Often, we supplied their first communication to the outside. Logging camps, hospitals, fish canneries, fish camps, and isolated personal holdings had all laboured for years with no communication other than the slow mails. Transportation had been limited to coastal steamers, mainly the Union Steamships vessels. To fly into an isolated camp with a recent newspaper was an event.

Completing a radio telephone installation and handing the handset to someone in camp was an exciting experience for both participants. When reception conditions permitted, calls could be placed in and out of camp. Business could be conducted quickly. Personal calls improved morale. Everyone on the coast listened in to these radio calls, a community was formed, information was shared up and down the coast.

Often you were dropped off on a boom of logs somewhere to await pick-up by the camp crew. Proper meals and beds could not be counted on. You couldn't leave until you established or restored radio communications into Vancouver Northwest Telephone, whose radio operators would patch calls in (connect them through the land-line network) to the desired number.

When Jim Spilsbury brought in Jack Tindall as a third partner, Jim Hepburn moved his shares to QCA, taking over the airline radio work. The radio firm's name became Spilsbury & Tindall Ltd.

Jack Tindall was a self-made entrepreneur, having established a thriving up-coast store and supply centre at Refuge Cove, north of Powell River. Jack was used to a slow pace; the time of day or pressures of the moment were of little concern to him. He was committed to his work and available at all times to all, but sadly unable to adapt to a faster, less personal pace of business.

I proposed we establish a properly functioning service department: use specific work orders, put an end to workers drifting in and out as they pleased, keep an inventory record, and above all, establish a working invoicing system. They agreed and I was appointed sales and service manager.

New people were added, some left, and we went ahead with new radio designs. A small assembly line manufactured marine and land radiophones and Spilsbury & Tindall products were becoming the first choice of users on the B.C. coast and farther afield.

As a former lowly leading aircraftsman, and a young one at that, I needed considerable tact to direct my ex-air force flight sergeant and other former officers now working for me on Civvie Street. The tact had to be learned; it was not a skill that flourished in my family. However, I did find a natural instinct working for me, that of marketing. Quite a change from the air force where the ability to conform was a key factor.

Northwest Telephone Company, a subsidiary of B.C. Telephone Company, had the monopoly on radiotelephone connections with the land telephone system. All camps and boats had to contact B.C. Telephone's Vancouver or Prince Rupert radio operators to be patched into the land telephone system. Even camp-to-camp communication was not permitted – calls had to be routed through the phone company and this was nearly impossible because of the limited hours of radio wave propagation. Compare this with today, when it is possible for aircraft radios to scan and connect to many frequencies.

It was technically illegal at the time, but out of desperation, we put our heads together and installed in the Stranraers a marine radiotelephone that allowed them to talk to fishboats and tugboats and to phone in to the Northwest Telephone network.

Many times I would be seated in the cockpit calling a Vancouver operator while airborne, pressing the headphones to hear better, only to be told: "Stand by, there are calls ahead of you." We finally solved this difficulty with the telephone company by identifying our call as an aircraft communication, so as to be put through immediately, before arriving at our destination.

Eventually the Department of Transport assigned 6495

*Sullivan Bay Float Camp in 1951 was typical of coastal camps. Easy to build, no land to clear and simple to move. Just attach a cable and tow to a new location. Sullivan Bay, a pivotal centre for coastal air and water traffic, was owned and operated by Bruce and Myrtle Collinson. Photo Credit: Bruce Collinson Collection.*

khz as our airline frequency, which gave us good coastal coverage. Permission was then granted to establish base sets in Vancouver and Prince Rupert and install the frequencies in up-coast camps. We designed a five-watt radiotelephone that was dropped off at camps where business warranted. Now with radios along the coast the airline could gather weather information and the aircraft could be in contact most of the time. There was still no aircraft-to-boat communication, something we would have found reassuring in the event of a forced landing in rough waters.

Establishing these small stations was history repeating

itself. During the war, the air force had scows at points on the coast gathering weather information and feeding information continually into Western Air Command near Jericho Beach, where my wife Jean was an air force wireless operator collecting this information hourly.

The scows were equipped with a wireless operator, a technician and a cook-mechanic to look after the generating plant and keep the scow afloat. Every few weeks an air force supply boat appeared with mail and supplies. Airmen were allowed on board the supply boat for a few beers before it sailed on to the next stop. Some scows were very isolated with only forest paths ashore to native or other small settlements.

## New Times – New Ways

The QCA Stranraers on the coastal runs carried 20 passengers and three crew members. Passengers were seated, mostly without seatbelts, on long benches broadside, facing each other and the aluminum shell. First-time passengers were alarmed at the deafening noise from the hull during landing and takeoff, especially in rough weather. The flight engineer, reconnecting the starter batteries on the floor from parallel to series with a wrench on each takeoff, did little to bolster passenger confidence. Later we remedied this electrical problem.

Flights were frequently rowdy; disputes and quarrels

*Stranraer flying boats were the workhorses for more than two decades on the British Columbia Coast. There is a story that an Air Force Strannie on patrol sighted a U.S. Convoy about 100 miles out to sea on its way to Alaska. To be friendly, the Strannie flew over the convoy in greeting only to be met by gunfire. It seems the Americans figured only the Japanese could be flying such a relic. Photo Credit: RCAF Collection.*

grew proportionate to the rounds of the bottle. One flight engineer used his large crescent wrench to threaten unruly loggers.

Toilet facilities were in the former tail gunner's compartment. It was an open area covered with a tarp, so passengers, after climbing up to the tail, got privacy by pulling the tarp across the entranceway. The tarp would flap in the slipstream, and I remember people started calling the Strannies the Whistling Outhouses. The flight engineer had the job of emptying the honey bucket into the sea after we landed.

But the lack of comfort was well compensated by the speed of travel. When the sea was not too rough, passengers

90

could be transferred to any bobbing tender that would come out to meet the aircraft.

Baggage had to be handed out of the nose section in front of the cockpit. Most pilots helped with baggage, others, mentally still in the air force, walked away after landing, leaving it for the flight engineer. I had to rush to do the radio work, but at times helped too. Refuelling was done from aviation fuel tanks at the oil companies' tank sites set up for the marine craft.

There were many close calls and mixups, some of them even funny. One involved Jim Hepburn. He had finished his radio repairs at a cannery on Vancouver Island's west coast, placed all his parts and tools in a cardboard box, then sat on the dock awaiting the arrival of the flying boat. The aircraft taxied in to the float. Hepburn picked up his box and proceeded to walk down the float watching the aircraft taxiing in. He became focused on the aircraft and walked right off the float into the water. The crew hauled him out. His box of testers and parts was floating but when lifted out of the water, the wet bottom let go, and out went all the contents. Luckily, they landed on the float, not in the drink.

Most of the trips up-coast were on short notice and the weather on many occasions was very unpleasant. It became routine: take off in the rain, clouds, poor visibility, Sunshine Coast to your right, Stillwater water tower, Powell River smoke, the sandy beaches of Savary Island and then a string of islands and entrances to inlet after inlet, like the fingers on your hand.

*Louis aboard the Seiner Freeland. It was common for the "Radio Man" to hitch rides from camp to camp. Many a party was celebrated along the way.*

Usually we were flying at low altitude, hugging the shoreline in extremely bad weather, circling the camp to alert them to send out a boat to meet the plane. If no boats were spotted, you were deposited on a log boom until someone came to take you to shore. Being dropped off on a rolling log boom didn't occur to us as being dangerous, although I couldn't swim, and had a deep fear of water for many years, having almost drowned at the age of 10. My mother said at the time that I didn't drown because I was born with a veil over my head.

Often I arranged for a camp boat to take me to another location, working my way from inlet to inlet or island to island until I was able to board a steamer for the city or pick up a flight back. Frequently on the steamship, I settled down for the night on a pile of laundry bags.

Canadian Fishing Company (CANFISCO) was one of

our major customers. Each year, we journeyed to each of its cannery sites to set up the radio equipment for the fishing season. In those days, we serviced Bones Bay (near Alert Bay), Goose Bay in Rivers Inlet, Margaret Bay in Smith Inlet, Kildala camp, an arm of Rivers Inlet, Butedale Cannery on Princess Royal Island.

During canning season at Butedale Cannery, the water into the bay would be pink with blood from the cutting tables. The fish guts were shovelled onto a scow, towed out to sea and dumped. The seagull activity was fierce, the gulls covered the scow and screamed like bedlam.

Seiners from all the fishing companies would tie up at Butedale on their way to the fishing grounds, some needing radio repairs. Butedale had a lot of radiotelephone traffic to Vancouver, which was augmented by a wireless operator sending radio telegrams via the government station at Port Hardy and then on to the Canadian National in Vancouver. The wireless operator kept watch on all the channels; the radio room was a busy place receiving and relaying messages.

Flare-ups among bored passengers on the Union steamship line occurred frequently during long trips that offered no entertainment other than the bottle in the shared stateroom. One spring trip to the opening of the Goose Bay Cannery at Rivers Inlet was no exception. Aboard were two ruffians from Quebec getting drunker as time passed.

The ship carried a large number of Chinese cannery

workers who kept to themselves in their quarters below deck but small groups would parade around the ship for fresh air. Our two ruffians were dispensing racial slurs to the Chinese as they passed. When one of them staggered and fell over the transom, the insults were returned loudly in Chinese, together with several tough body kicks. Other passengers nearby clapped their hands.

At the cannery the Chinese had their own camp abundantly decorated with bottom fish drying for winter food back in Vancouver. Local native workers with their families occupied cabins formerly used by Japanese before the war.

My next call was Campbell Island, now Bella Bella proper, to the W.R. Large Memorial Hospital on the Indian Reserve, operated by the United Church. I arrived, repaired the hospital radiotelephone, and sold a marine radiotelephone to Dr. George Darby, the medical officer, for the boat he used for emergency calls.

I awaited the radio's arrival on the freighter, installed it on the vessel, and got a lift to Namu with a rheumatic fisherman who lived on his small boat with his cat. He told me he hadn't been to Vancouver since 1911, 37 years before.

In Namu I jumped aboard the Charmaine C, the last of the steam-powered vessels owned by Canfisco, and we had a slow trip up North Bentinck Arm, accompanied by a huge whale.

I remember being surprised at Tallyho Cannery, on North Bentinck Arm. The manager was a tough old guy,

Quisenberry, whose first name nobody seemed to know. In the office was a large sheet of pre-war plywood painted white. It had rows of hooks on it, each with a boat number. The first row was labelled "white" in large block letters. The next row was labelled "Japs" and the last row "Indians."

I was shocked at the racist designations, and asked about it. It was his record of boat assignments. He no longer had any "Japs." Their column of hooks was now filled with "Indians". Quisenberry said he would take the "Japs" back any day because they were producers. This too startled me as I was still carrying the mental baggage of Japanese as enemies in the war.

No return aircraft was available so I made my way back to Ocean Falls on a small bakery boat. This fellow baked bread on his boat and called in at the camps regularly. The distances were far apart and I couldn't see his enterprise blossoming. The B.C. coast was populated with many like him, escaping the city for reasons unknown and supporting themselves with private endeavours and a little fishing.

Once the Stranraer flying boat picked me up in Ocean Falls and aboard was Jim Hepburn, returning from radio work at Stewart, just across the B.C. border from the Alaskan Panhandle. It was a perfectly clear day, so Andy Anderson, the pilot, decided to fly inland over the mountains, taking the direct route to Vancouver.

What a contrast to the cloud and turbulence of our usual low-altitude flights, to be flying above a panorama of glaci-

95

er-studded mountains!

Hep and I chatted away as Andy appeared, carrying his canvas money bag, collecting cash, vouchers and tickets. Hep was startled and asked who was flying the plane. He was told it was on automatic pilot. But we knew the automatic pilot was just a steel bar wedged in place on the control column to keep the elevators and rudder level.

There was no aircraft heat, no blankets, just the aluminum skin of the aircraft to keep out the cold. And it was cold on the 90 mph trip home. (They used to say the Stranraers took off, cruised and landed at 90 miles an hour.)

Sullivan Bay, 1951

*An air view of Sullivan Bay in 1951*
*Countless bays up and down the coast harboured similar floating communities.*
*Photo credit: Bruce Collinson Collection*

The mid-coast transportation hub was Sullivan Bay, owned and operated by Bruce and Myrtle Collinson. Here, freight boats unloaded supplies for outlying logging camps to be picked up by camp tenders, QCA aircraft refuelled and picked up passengers.

Spilsbury & Tindall installed radio communication and it soon became a thriving drop-off centre and passenger exchange for small boats and light planes.

When QCA was flying to the Queen Charlotte Islands, one of the most meticulous pilots in the air was Art Barran. Art was pleasant and full of energy, even after numerous stops on the trip up. One evening at the Sandspit Pacific Mills camp, Art and the superintendent were playing bridge with some others. I walked along the beach near the bunkhouses to get Art to turn in for the night. A great storm was brewing and the wind picked me up, so I took a couple of steps in mid-air with each gust. But Art, always pretty casual, just expressed his hope the Anson hadn't blown away.

Next morning there was more than a foot of snow on the airstrip, and Art had to taxi back and forth to beat the snow down. But we took off and were out of the weather in clear skies at about 700 feet. The winds were too strong for us to make a refuelling stop at Port Hardy, so we flew on past Powell River. A gust of wind ripped the plywood inspection panel off the wing, leaving a gaping hole, but we landed

uneventfully in Vancouver.

Kenny McQuaig was another pilot I spent time with. He had commanded a squadron of Sunderland flying boats in the Royal Canadian Air Force in England when he was only 21 years old. I was on the Norseman with Kenny one day when we had to pick up passengers at Minstrel Island.

The wind was blowing up waves which made it impossible to taxi in to the float, and we had to wait, bobbing on the water and starting the engine every so often to keep from drifting ashore. Finally a small rowboat made its way out with three passengers for us. But there was no way we could get them aboard, so we asked the rower to bring them back in a larger boat.

Back they came on the deck of a small, short-masted fishboat and we got a rope on it but the wind rocked the Norseman, lifting the wing and pulling the boat forward. Then the wing swung down, to be pierced by the boat's mast. What a dilemma! We were drifting around, plane and boat locked together as one.

The rowboat man came back out to help and we sent him

back again for a handsaw. Rusty and dull as it was, and having to balance carefully, we managed to saw the mast off at its base, freeing the boat from the wing. Then we pulled the mast out of the wing, out came the fabric patching kit, and we hastily patched the top wing surface in a rather unorthodox manner. We figured that should give us lift so we left the hole in the bottom of the wing as it was, and took off for Vancouver. Another day in the life of a flying radio man.

Flying with Bill Peters one time, we were low on gas. Bill spotted a small fishing vessel near Lund north of Powell River, landed and taxied up to the surprised fisherman and asked if he would take me in as he was low on fuel and wanted to lighten the plane. I had a huge salmon on board which Bill flew home and delivered to my wife that evening. Luckily I caught the midnight sailing of the CN steamer from Powell River to Vancouver, enjoying for once the comfort of a stateroom.

I also flew often with Jim's cousin Rupert Spilsbury and chief pilot and operations manager Johnny Hatch. Rupert, an ex-Ferry Command pilot, had been instrumental in getting Jim started in owning aircraft.

Passenger traffic increased steadily and QCA outgrew the Stranraers and Ansons to fly Catalina (Canso) flying boats, DC3s and other aircraft, flown by airline-trained pilots accustomed to flying from A to B in a routine manner.

Bill Sylvester, founder of BC Airlines, took over all the up-coast feeder services to feed into the QCA points like

*Displaying radio-telephone, MRT-25, typical of the hundreds made by Spilsbury and Tindall and sold to vessels on the Pacific, Atlantic and Arctic Coasts. An additional popular feature was their standard AM receiver dial.*

Tofino, Comox, Port Hardy. It was a big undertaking to get the newly acquired BCA frequency installed in the many up-coast radio telephones in service. The job was taken on by our technician, Les Payne, who later disappeared in the Cessna he was flying to Prince Rupert with my buddy and assistant Brian Stevenson.

Brian Stevenson was one of my close associates at Spilsbury & Tindall. We travelled together at times on company sales projects. Many evenings on the road we talked about the numerous air accidents and close calls and the inherent dangers of flying under coastal weather conditions. We talked about acquaintances who had lost their lives. We felt it was a pretty risky business and felt lucky no one in our radio group had perished. How ironic.

After I left the company, it came as a gut shock to me when, at Lillooet Lake, I heard on the CKNW news that Brian Stevenson, salesman, and Les Payne, technician and hobby pilot, were lost on the coast. Their small wheeled aircraft had crashed into the sea on a flight from Vancouver to Prince Rupert.

They were on their way to Prince Rupert to demonstrate new radio equipment to the telephone company. They stopped at Port Hardy and then disappeared over the water.

Their loss struck at my heart. I had hired both men and worked with them over the years. Why did they not take a commercial flight when it was available? How could this happen in a company with years of flying experience? With floats, they would have had a chance.

## A Change of Scene

Not all our installations were on the coast. In 1948 the Hope-Princeton Highway was under construction, crossing the mountains from the rainforest coast to the dry interior of British Columbia.

Looking forward to a pleasant change of scene, Brian and I left Vancouver by car about 4 a.m., loaded with batteries, radiotelephone and wire antenna to install at a mine south of the Hope-Princeton Highway. The highway had been built only some 25 miles from Hope and we were instructed to turn off to the base camp up the valley. This being a Sunday morning, most of the staff and crew were away.

The cook rounded up a packer who packed four horses with our equipment while we watched with admiration. Later, he brought out two riding horses. A few of the workers looked on with interest and laughed when I positioned my horse opposite the cookhouse porch, so I could mount.

We were told: "Follow the horses, but be sure they don't leave the trail, or they will attempt to brush off their load. Also be sure you keep them tied up or they will leave you at the mine and return to the barn at the bottom of the mountain."

I rode the lead horse, Brian the last, to keep our pack train intact. Sure enough, some horses veered into the bush. Brian had to back them up to the trail. We came to a rock slide with a very narrow passage jam-packed with rocks. It was like riding a camel, so I dismounted and walked in front. But it was rough going, so I remounted, finding the horse more sure-footed on the foot-wide trail.

We had been warned to take this slide area carefully, as some horses had lost their footing and rolled down to their death. However, we managed to arrive without incident, double-tied the horses and unpacked our gear at the empty camp. Brian climbed the trees and rigged two aerials. Before long, we were able to phone Jack Tindall in Vancouver and report success.

The view south from the mountaintop looked toward the U.S.A., the view west to Vancouver Island. However, we had no time to savour the view – the horses were anxious to be fed and watered. The return trip was swift and wild. When we reached the valley floor, our horses were in full gallop and it was all Brian and I could do to hold on until we pulled up at the barn.

Radio men will like this one. Emil Anderson Construction Company had the contract to build the Hope-Princeton Highway to the summit. The Department of Transport assigned 1698 khz as the frequency for inter-camp use. Any radio man will know such a low frequency at five watts of power is useless in the mountains. Jim Hepburn couldn't get the link to work, so he removed a few turns of wire from the coils, tuned the equipment to the second harmonic on 2396 khz and with the power reduced to 2.5 watts, established communications, figuring it would not likely bother anyone.

Winter was soon upon us and Campbell Manix Construction was building the John Hart Highway from Prince George to Summit Lake and on to Dawson Creek. We had the contract to manufacture and install radiotelephones for all three locations. I flew to Prince George on the Canadian Pacific night flight and checked in to the Patricia Hotel. Prince George wasn't much in those days, a building here and there with lots of vacant land. The wooden sidewalk creaked with frozen snow as I tramped my way to the construction camp.

We rigged up the Prince George station and took off at

night with the company's refurbished Anson, landing on a newly cleared snow strip at Summit Lake. We had only the aircraft lights to see us in. It was cold, very cold. The plane left us there to do the installation and the next day it came back to take us on another night flight to Fort St. John. Once there we wheeled the aircraft into the hangar, drained the oil to prevent freezing up, and headed off to the hotel for a few hours' sleep.

The next day we were taken to the Dawson Creek camp. It was still extremely cold. I finished that installation, connecting the three sites by radio and it worked, because the frequency assigned was a suitable one. Everyone was satisfied and I had enjoyed seeing one more portion of B.C.'s new highway system taking shape.

The following summer, I was back flying the coast again in the Waco floatplane, now part of the QCA fleet.

### A Big Contract

One major project we had was providing communication for the Alcan engineers who were to spend the winter on a glacier-covered area between Kemano and Kitimat to study the feasibility of a power line. We supplied a one-watt radiophone and trained people to use it. This allowed them to receive and send spoken radiograms via the government station at Bull Harbour on the tip of Vancouver Island. The radio performed so well, they recommended us to Morrison

Knudsen, the Kemano contractors. I sold them over $125,000 worth of radio equipment for the project, big money in 1954.

During this period, a Queen Charlotte Airlines night flight from Kitimat to Vancouver crashed on Mount Benson near Nanaimo, with all the Alcan Kitimat directors aboard. The fallout from this dreadful accident tarnished QCA's reputation and the association between Jim Spilsbury, president of Queen Charlotte Airlines, and the Spilsbury & Tindall radio company was too close for us. So the radio company started to distance itself from the airline.

After 12 years with the company, Jack Tindall, who had always been a chain smoker, died of cancer and I lost my mentor. The subsequent changes in the company gave rise to a separate sales company, S. & T. Sales Ltd., which I headed as managing director. I was grateful that Jack had shared his knowledge of commerce with me. Although laid-back and casual, Jack introduced me to office and corporate procedure, and together we helped the company prosper.

Alex Itenson was the creator of the company's regular production line. Alex, a White Russian, had come to us by way of Hong Kong where he had been a prisoner of the Japanese during the war. At Spilsbury & Tindall, one of his promising factory workers was Winnie Hope, who later became the second wife of Jim Spilsbury. Years later, Alex left the company with my secretary in tow for better opportunities in Ottawa.

Alex had a talent for exterior design for our radiotele-phones which added style and function to our product. His chassis and panel design continued to be popular for many more years.

Every small provincial airline called on us for radio com-munications equipment. We had now become adept in obtaining frequencies for these carriers. Russ Baker's Pacific Western Airlines, QCA's future rival, purchased our equipment. I recall installing equipment in Russ' Cessna Crane before Central BC Airlines became PWA. Russ was in coveralls polishing the wings and neither of us had any idea at that time that PWA would eventually take over QCA.

Transmountain Pipeline called on us for high-frequency communications equipment for the Edmonton-to-Vancouver oil pipeline. B.C. Electric Company, expanding its transmission lines from Bridge River to Vancouver, called on us for HF mobile equipment and several base stations. Canadian National Railways was having trouble moving trains in the Fraser Canyon during telegraph line outages. We supplied the railway division with five-watt radiotele-phones at numerous stations in the Fraser Canyon, operat-ing on 1698 khz.

The system would not have worked except that the wire antennae were mounted on telegraph poles so the signal was carried along by induction. It moved the trains, to the sur-prise of the Canadian National chief of telegraph operations, who felt we had invaded his turf.

Those years gave me wonderful experience in getting along with all walks of people. Much of our expansion was due to good products, made exactly to specifications I would relate to the factory after determining the customer's needs. We all worked as a team with Winnie Hope expediting the manufacturing process, making certain the product met the delivery date.

## We Say Good-Bye

After many years of unrelenting competition, QCA was sold to Pacific Western Airlines, its aggressive rival.

Queen Charlotte Airlines had been flying high, but morale was often shaky, as were finances. A series of investors had to be found, the last of whom was Frank Griffiths. He became a shareholder and comptroller of the company in the latter days of QCA operations. In 1956, when Pacific Western Airlines offered to purchase QCA, Frank Griffiths pushed the sale through in spite of opposition from the founders.

The capital from the sale enabled Griffiths to purchase CKNW in New Westminster from Bill Rae and build an empire of radio and television broadcasting stations known later as WIC (Western International Communications). Jim Spilsbury returned to the radio company.

After the sale of QCA, Jim was anxious to get reacquainted with the radio business. We went on a lower coast cruise aboard the company's Blithe Spirit, calling at many camps and ports Jim had frequented earlier in his radio repair days, fixing domestic radios out of Savary Island.

But the changes of modernization were being felt. The telephone company's VHF (very high frequency)

*A happy fellow posing for 1956 sales brochure. What could be better than selling our company-manufactured communications equipment throughout Canada?*

network was replacing Spilsbury & Tindall's high-frequency radios. Our sets were being relegated to points where VHF signals could not penetrate and microwave links were not in place. So it was agreed that if the company was to survive, we had to seek frontier markets across Canada and abroad. However, Jim's heart was in the B.C. coast and he did not play much of a role in our cross-Canada expansion.

We moved across Canada, supplying terminal equipment for B.C., Alberta, Manitoba, and Quebec, and in Newfoundland we supplied radio communications to the Grenfell Mission coastal outposts. We also supplied communications to the Newfoundland government for forestry, mining and highway construction as they pushed expansion after confederation.

One of the most satisfying contracts was with Bell

Telephone for six-channel sideband radiotelephones installed at Frobisher Bay and nine other Arctic locations, all of which fed into the continental telephone system at Alma, Quebec.

The Arctic became a considerable market, as we supplied communications to many outposts, the RCMP, government surveyors, Indian reservations and small airlines.

We tended to pursue hunches without extensive research. It rewarded us well, as we could respond quickly to clients' needs. It was a working framework where I had full freedom to perform. Had I failed, as many did, I would have been out of a job. For me, it was an opportunity to grow and I was grateful.

In the few short years I spent bringing radio communications to the B.C. coast, my life was enriched immeasurably by the camaraderie afforded me by QCA aircrews and the knowledge they shared freely.

Those who lost their lives pioneering air service on our wonderful but unpredictable coast are well remembered. Remembered too, my buddy and true friend Brian Stevenson, lost on that ill-fated flight up the coast.

*Brian Stevenson*
*Photo credit: Joyce Stevenson Collection*

# CHAPTER 5
# JAPAN

Our sales company at Spilsbury & Tindall was constant-ly on the lookout for new electronic products to market. Our interest was aroused in 1954 when the Japanese began to offer us radio components and small battery radios.

We sensed the ingenuity of the Japanese and thought these products would soon lead to more sophisticated items. We wanted to be connected to the product source. So my proposal to make a trip to Japan was readily agreed upon.

In the spring of 1955, with inner feelings of consorting with a former enemy, I boarded a Canadian Pacific Airlines plane in Vancouver bound for Tokyo. In Cold Bay, Alaska, our refuelling stop, I stepped off the plane and jumped back aboard, blown in by the wind and cold. There were only a few passengers on this 20-hour flight so we talked the time away.

*Manufacturers of electronics in Tokyo, 1956. All representatives had products they wished to export to Canada. On my left is the Commercial Trade Secretary from the Canadian Embassy. On my right is interpreter Miyabe San.*

I had corresponded with the Canadian Embassy in Tokyo and told them about my previous sales experience in South America, so the embassy had prepared my way. Japanese business representatives met me and took me directly to a meeting where I was introduced to manufacturers and asked to address a select group. I felt awkward when presented with a bouquet of roses, standing there without shoes, which I had been told to leave at the door.

A long line of eager exporters formed, and after a bow, each of them presented a business card. I collected several before realizing I couldn't read them. I had the interpreter write names and products on each card. Before long I had to stop the line to go to the men's room.

I was already feeling culture shock but was not prepared to see women entering and leaving the washroom. In trepidation, I too entered and immediately felt a bit more comfortable seeing the long horizontal urinal, just like in an air force barracks. Suddenly I panicked again, as I glanced to the left where a pretty Japanese lady was applying her makeup at the mirror next to the urinal. She paid no attention to me so I stared forward as I did my thing, zipped up and tried to act unconcerned. I now felt I had a grip and was ready for whatever came my way.

I went back and met the rest of the businessmen and we proceeded to another hall. Seated at the head table were a representative from the Canadian Embassy and representatives from the local export group promoting the event. With the help of an interpreter, I was introduced and the purpose of my visit explained.

They asked me to outline my experience, our company's history and the products we needed. What impressed them most was my young age, 31 years, and the growth of our company, Spilsbury & Tindall. Their eagerness was overwhelming and left no doubt in my mind of the manufacturing explosion about to take place.

## I Got the Royal Treatment

I was one of a few visiting Japan to promote trade at that time, and was being accorded the VIP treatment. As Japan's

exports expanded, future businessmen were not treated as royally.

My interpreter, Miyabe San, had an excellent command of the English language, having served before the war as the Japanese representative for Canadian Pacific Steamships and I couldn't help wondering what he did in the war. He liked to talk about Banff and Niagara Falls, a must for the Japanese tourists. His charming wife had attended university in prewar California.

*Japanese characters depicting Potvin San.*

I set out to learn a few Japanese words and phrases. I couldn't figure out why everyone said "mushi-mushi" upon answering the phone and frequently used the words "ah sodeska" during conversations. It's easy when you know, mushi-mushi is hello, hello, and ah-sodeska has many forms of meaning like "is that so?" or is used as an acknowledgement of some kind. I soon learned to respond to my last name Potvin, pronounced in Japanese "Pot-o-veen," followed by the word "san" to indicate a closeness, familiarity or respect.

We visited many large factories and many smaller family-operated ones. The larger firms sent a car to my hotel, Nikatsu, to pick me up. The white-gloved chauffeurs polished the door handle and seat before I entered the shiny, black, prewar vehicle that looked as if it should carry royalty. It was like going back in time. I felt important but wondered if I would live up to expectations.

Mini taxis were everywhere. In downtown Tokyo you could hail a taxi in a moment. The Ginza, Tokyo's main street, had developed to serve the U.S. occupation forces and the Japanese men as well. The proliferation of neon signs and the number of nightclubs were astounding. I was taken to the Kabuki Theatre. I enjoyed the performance, with the interpreter whispering English in my ear. The show portrayed an early invasion of Korea with the heavy casualties acted out graphically. Everything had deep meaning and sorrow, the music reinforcing the mood.

I was invited to a social gathering where, perhaps to please me, the men wore top hats and tails, a dress that was prevalent in the pre-war era but now out of date.

### Factories and Piecework

The large factories were just like any other back in North America, except all the workers wore white smocks, white head dress and many wore a face mask over mouth and nose.

A factory worker entered the hall in front of our entourage one day. The head

*Miyabe San in front of the Nikatsu Hotel in Tokyo. For my four week stay Miyabe was interpreter, guide and friend.*

115

of the company delegation ran ahead and pushed her forcibly against the wall. Her action was perceived as disrespect. The tone of his voice left no doubt what he said to her. She bowed as we went by. I smiled in return.

This didn't sit well with me, but I reminded myself this was another country, another social structure and I was a guest.

I also saw small family concerns that made components. Frequently there were small plants on the street level with the family living upstairs. What was interesting was there was no office to see, everyone worked on production and records were kept upstairs in the home. We all sat on the floor, drank saki and were served choice dishes from the few foods available on the market.

One such visit was to a condenser factory being re-established from prewar beginnings. The owner had a model of the warship he commanded during the war and took great pains and pride in explaining it to me. Having been in the air force, I found it difficult to adjust to the new relationship, but could see the former naval man had long ago passed that stage.

*Rincan Company owner discussing their product, a miniature tube portable radio. We introduced it in Canada, the first of its kind in the country.*

I found it embarrassing going to the family bathroom, a wooden-panelled room with a sink, mirror and a hole in the floor. I looked down the hole and saw a very large porcelain tub. The young daughter, 15 or 16 years old, waited with a hot, steamy face cloth and towel which she used to help dry my hands. It was not the unfamiliar culture that was awkward, it was the fear of being disrespectful or doing the wrong thing.

I did make one goof, when I asked what the men pulling wagons down the street were doing. I was told, "You know, the honey bucket." If they had said the chamber pot, I would have understood right away. They were embarrassed to explain that central sewage pipes did not exist in many areas of Tokyo. The honey bucket patrol exchanged these very large porcelain chamber pots from each home on a regular basis.

Our visits took me to many well-known electronic names of today, Pioneer, Oki-Denki, Sony, Kenwood, known as Trio at the time of my visit. I also visited NHK, the national broadcasting system where Tokyo Rose made her broadcasts during World War II.

When visiting larger plants, we entered the tea room and were served tea. The receptionist was like a hostess. Evenings were taken up wining and dining, and business was discussed late into the night, with the help of saki and beer. It was a very busy schedule and keeping notes on my activities became a time-consuming job. I established representation for many products and felt the trip well worthwhile.

117

Our visit to the Sony factory held no special interest, surprising as that may seem today. It was a small plant. My first impression upon entering was of a tea-stained table cloth, an unusual sight in Japan. I had tea and was shown a small, hand-held, portable AM radio. It was a feat in miniaturization. The battery lasted four hours. I informed them I had just agreed to represent another make.

Then the engineer brought out a mini TV set using a round picture tube. It was an impressive design but I felt round picture tubes wouldn't sell. The reason round TV tubes were used is that these were the cathode ray tubes made for test equipment that were available to the engineers.

The first TV sets people in Vancouver bought had featured round picture tubes, but they were soon replaced by rectangular tubes.

I've been kidded about it since, but couldn't see any benefit in representing Sony. I felt they didn't have anything more to offer than the companies we were to represent. My old friend Ron calls me the guy who turned down a chance to become a multi-millionaire, but I have no regrets. Our small operation could never have filled the future needs of Sony as they leaped ahead in the market.

I'm not envious of the success of Sony today, but my early glimpse into the Japanese ingenuity and drive painted a picture of what was to come.

One manufacturer invited me to Hakone Hot Springs for the weekend. When breakfast time came, I was asked what I would like to eat. I said bacon, eggs and toast. There was considerable discussion and a boy was sent some seven miles by bicycle to locate eggs and bacon. An hour and a half later, I had my breakfast, now feeling foolish for not realizing Western-type food was still very expensive and scarce in Japan.

*At Hakoni Hot Springs all guests were supplied with personal kimonos. This is the site of my big faux pas at which I requested bacon and eggs for breakfast.*

To have marketed the consumer products the Japanese were to offer would have been a distinct departure from our normal business. It would have called for a type of marketing expertise we did not have. I suggested to Spilsbury we could take advantage of the contacts I had made in Japan and look for an investor-manager of such an operation. But this did not materialize.

When the time came to depart, our flight was delayed three hours, but there were over 150 men and women with

119

umbrellas braving the rain on the rooftop waving their good-byes as my plane taxied out. It was a very touching experience.

I also had to cope with the many gifts that were heaped upon me. They were all put in a large container and shipped home separately, to be cleared through Canadian Customs a few days after my return to Vancouver.

Back at the plant, after some debriefing, we established S. & T. Sales (Import) Ltd. to market Japanese products. We flooded the electronic supply houses with various radio parts, numerous electrical testers, panel meters, PVC tape, radio kits for schools, portable radios and a variety of other items. We sold this line profitably for years until we decided to concentrate on manufacturing and selling our own communications equipment.

# CHAPTER 6
## LILLOOET LAKE

Here is the place that is dear to my heart. When in 1958 I fell in love with our stretch of waterfront on Lillooet Lake, I didn't realize how much of my life it would take up.

Family trailering weekends had whetted our appetite for a piece of land of our own where we would not have to wonder if camp space were available.

Work at Spilsbury & Tindall was intense, with long hours. So we tried to get away on weekends, all four of us, Jean and I, our daughter Heather, nine, and our son Bruce, seven.

In the mid-'50s I had noticed the holiday trailers American tourists were driving, in particular the 15-foot Shasta, easily manageable and suitable for a family of four. The Vancouver representative had one in stock for me to view. It was a beauty, with yellow sides, white roof, double bed, folding bunk, breakfast nook that could be made into a bunk, propane stove and icebox. A recent raise had persuaded us to buy a brand-new Chevy Bel-air sedan, custom-painted black and red sides with white roof. A wonderful vehicle. Together, the car and trailer made an eye-catching combination.

I installed a propane heater and a better radio that didn't need replacement batteries, and rigged a battery in the trailer, charged by the car, so we always had lights. This was

*Our treasured Bel Air and Trailer on one of our first trips exploring southern British Columbia in 1956. These travels soon stimulated a search for our own piece of wilderness.*

before the manufacturers built in such conveniences as original equipment. With such an efficient outfit, our family took off every weekend we could. With the heater, we were able to use the trailer until late November.

It was truly an exciting time. There weren't many campsites in those days, but we got to Emory Creek, upstream past Hope on the Fraser River, to the Gold Pan campsite on the sandy shore of the Thompson River, to campsites on the Hope-Princeton Highway and, on three-day weekends, to the Antlers campsite on Okanagan Lake.

We even motored to my birthplace, Bonnyville, 175 miles northeast of Edmonton. It was a shock to see no sign of life in the place of my childhood memories. The water table had shrunk so much, our one-mile lake was dry and covered with golden wheat fields.

The years having taken their toll, even relatives were scarce. But we parked the car and trailer at my second cousin Orphelia's farm. It didn't take him long to notify others of my French-Canadian clan. Many of them dropped in to see us, and I was surprised to see my old schoolteacher, Henri Bourgoin, who called without knowing I was there.

We rediscovered a warm relationship which lasted for many more years, with him and his wife (my second cousin Lucienne) coming out to visit us when we got established at Lillooet Lake; and with us going back to Bonnyville many times later. He was glad to know Jean, who, though born in Scotland, was educated at Westmount High in Montreal, where he had also been a student.

All our travels were interesting but I wanted to settle closer to home. I had done a lot of travel on the B.C. coast by boat and aircraft in the late 1940s and early 1950s, and knew that the inaccessibility of up-coast locations ruled them out as a weekend retreat.

We also looked at the Sunshine Coast, then served by Blackball Ferries, but soon realized this was not the direction to take either.

Jim Spilsbury had organized a Queen Charlotte Airlines retreat at Garibaldi Lake, but it was accessible only by air and this held no promise for me. "Why don't you look beyond the Garibaldi area?" he asked. And I remember, he added: "There is bound to be a road into that area someday. And someday someone may start up a ski lodge."

What prophetic words! Now, Whistler is one of the most vibrant communities in B.C.

Searching in the Vancouver Sun, I came across a small ad reading "Pemberton Valley Farms, Pemberton, B.C." I wrote inquiring if a small piece of farm land might be available, pointing out my preference for an acre or two with a stream or better, a lake which I supposed was not a realistic expectation. Well, a letter came back advising there is such a place, 3/4-mile lakeshore, 128 acres on Lillooet Lake, a World War I soldiers' land grant. "The owner wants $1,500 for it," the agent wrote. "I have a notion to buy it myself for my own family." Bob Taylor was the agent, an early Pemberton Valley settler who knew how to hustle and make a dollar.

There was no road from the Coast to Pemberton in those days, but I knew a bit about the area. We had sold radio communications equipment to the B.C. Electric Co. – the forerunner of B.C. Hydro – and I was familiar with Squamish, having supplied two-way radio to logging operations years earlier.

I was also familiar with the B.C. Electric powerline from Bridge River to Vancouver via Pemberton, and a second line down Lillooet Lake as well, having supplied communications equipment to it and to Fleetwood Logging Co. on Lillooet Lake.

Lillooet Lake adjoins the Pemberton Valley and gold seekers going to the Cariboo travelled between 1858 and

1864 via Harrison, Lillooet, Anderson and Seton Lakes, with portages in between. It was the main route until the tortuous Fraser Canyon road was completed.

This was the Douglas Trail, as many as five sternwheelers plying Lillooet Lake. Parts of the steamer Prince of Wales are still to be seen at what was Port Pemberton, up on the Birkenhead River, which runs into Lillooet Lake. I have one of the boiler bricks, stamped "Newton." I assume it was made at Newton, B.C., now part of Surrey. They say you can still hear the ghosts of the paddle steamers on a still night.

I called the number, Pemberton 1B, it rang once and I heard a voice answering weakly through the nearly-overpowering hum on the line. We made a date and on May 10, 1958, we were met at the Pemberton rail station.

## Getting There is Half the Fun

It was one of the hottest days on record. I stepped off the train and immediately liked Pemberton, surrounded by sky-reaching snow-capped mountains and the feel of dryness in the air. Pemberton is just on the fringe of the coastal belt where the climate change is noticeable.

We climbed into Bob Taylor's four-wheel-drive pick-up,

me sitting outside on the loose spare tire, being thrown around as we tackled the rough road to the head of Lillooet Lake. The one-lane jeep road down the lake had been constructed jointly between Fleetwood Logging Company and the B.C. Electric Company, built to take in materials for the hydro line that had been completed just a few years before.

Some portions of the road were exceptionally steep with a sheer drop into the lake. In all my flying up the coast, air turbulence and all, I had not experienced anything as bouncy as this. Creeks were flowing across the road, and we stopped frequently to clear off rocks.

Initially, I thought this was no place for us. But Bob, a charmer, had my wife convinced this would soon be the future highway to Pemberton from Harrison Lake. He pointed out it had been the major trail in the gold rush era. He told her about the sternwheelers that had carried prospectors and entire mule trains with supplies up the lake. Bob told her it would be only a matter of time before we would have a highway at our door. It had to come, he said.

Finally we arrived at the property, eight kilometres down the lake (it was five miles in those days).

The veteran, Harry McCullough, still held it. He had to pay only $10 for it as a soldier's grant and he hadn't done much to improve it. The man who surveyed the land for Harry told him he had studied the whole lake and this was the best spot: a southern exposure, two running creeks and an area where mild weather prevailed.

A soldier friend of Harry's claimed the adjacent land, a beautiful sandy beach area. This veteran stayed on the property until the early 1930s, when he was getting on in years and went back to Ontario to be with family.

His property reverted to the Crown for unpaid taxes, which were only a few dollars a year at the time. I am proud to say that when we bought our property we suggested to the Parks Branch that the neighbouring sandy beach would make an excellent park, and a park reserve was placed on it. It was named Strawberry Point because the old soldier had grown strawberries on the sandy soil. It is now popular with campers and swimmers.

But I am getting ahead of my story.

The entrance to the lakeshore property was an overgrown trail. The truck drove down, gently bending over the small tree growth as we went.

## A Postcard Picture

We were enthralled at our first glimpse. The glacier-fed lake was calm, emerald green. We could hear the waterfall across the lake. The surrounding mountains were among the most scenic I had ever seen.

The beauty and tranquility settled over us. Except for the devastation made by loggers and the powerline builders, the place was just beautiful.

Fleetwood Logging had located a float camp on the shoreline and logged the area by A-frame, dragging the logs down the hillside and gouging everything along the way. This was the way it was done in the early days, when everyone figured there was a lot of B.C. left over.

Then the B.C. Electric cleared a 200-foot right-of-way for the powerline across the hillside, leaving tree debris all along the route.

It was not a pretty sight, but Jean and I fell in love with the lake and mountains and felt that the man-made scars would grow over. We decided to buy it, sit on it and find ways to use it.

The price was all of $1,500, Taylor having promised Harry $750 out of the proceeds of the sale. I negotiated terms of $500 down, $500 more in six months and the other $500 in 12 months.

*Bruce and Jean enjoying our very first view of Lillooet Lake. We fell in love and signed a purchase agreement that day, May 10, 1958*

*The old tool shed was the only building on the site when we purchased the property.*
*Fleetwood Logging had operated here when they logged portions of the lake.*
*Cabins from the float camp are still in use in Mount Currie.*

But Taylor, a wheeler-dealer, not a realtor, kept the first $500 payment and I believe there were a few harsh words spoken between the owner and Bob. When this appeared to be a problem, we borrowed the money and paid off the balance in full.

It must be realized the Pemberton Valley was cut off from road access to the city. People had to go by rail to Squamish and boat to Vancouver. Local money was hard to come by and city slickers entering the valley for the first time were looked upon as fat cats and easy prey, especially to unload some lands that flooded and were known to be infested with mosquitoes. The local people had not yet fully appreciated the thirst that had developed in the city for rural land.

*Our first summer at the lake, the yellow Shasta trailer was now paired with a large canvas tent. We were making our mark on the wilderness with a path to our door.*

My wife said she would break open her porcelain piggy bank and contribute and I promised to apply myself to earn the extra money to meet the payments. Six weeks after the purchase, I had enough extra to buy a 12-foot fibreglass boat from Davidson Co. at the entrance to Stanley Park. (What a great boat! It carried us four and our German Shepherd on many a trip around the lake.)

*Bruce and Heather sitting on an Indian dugout canoe with their catch of the day. Our first cabin on the beach is in the background, 1961.*

We shipped the boat, with a five-horsepower Johnson motor and our cherished trailer on a PGE flatcar, and had a local Pemberton fellow, Johnny Decker, haul it in with a small John Deere bulldozer. That was our big problem — the only way to get to

130

our place was by train to Pemberton and hire Bob Taylor to drive us down to the lake and pick us up before train time. This was expensive and he was not known for bargains.

During one of my lunches with Jim Spilsbury, we discussed my Lillooet Lake land acquisition. He said if I didn't want coastal property, I was in the right area. Later, while in Victoria on radio business, I was in the office of Phil Gaglardi, the Minister of Highways. Between telephone interruptions he said, "There is no doubt someday we will build a highway through the area, as a second route to the Interior is essential."

## The Mount Currie People

One of the secrets of the location is that to get to Lillooet Lake from Pemberton you have to pass through the Mount Currie Indian Reserve – they now proclaim it the Stl'Atl'Imx Territory of the Lil'Wat Nation.

Until quite recently you drove on a rutted gravel road that twisted for some eight kilometres or more along the Birkenhead River. Now, since the road has become part of the Duffy Lake highway to the town of Lillooet itself – another mountain range away – it is a seamless drive through unexpected pastoral vistas.

My son Bruce, seven at the time we set up our weekend retreat there in 1958, soon became enamoured of the native elders fishing at a camp they maintained on the border of the reserve at the head of the lake.

He made friends with Johnny and Susan Andrew, parents of Nick Andrew of rodeo fame, and Leonard and Fraser Andrew, who have both served as chiefs of the band.

The older Andrew lent Bruce two horses one summer, one for him to ride and one for his sister Heather. It was kindnesses like this that created a warm relationship between our families. Another oldtimer, Martin Williams, liked to hear young Bruce's stories of life in the city.

When we later set up permanent residence at the lake, Bruce, then 14, rode a motorbike part way to Pemberton High School, some 16 miles away. He would leave it on the reserve and get on the school bus with the Indian students. Later he was allowed to drive our four-wheel-drive vehicle to the reserve.

Lasting bonds were made with many of his schoolmates from Mount Currie and, years later, when we operated a

*Heather and Bruce riding the horses loaned to them for the summer by Johnny and Susan Andrew from Mount Currie.*

sawmill and planermill at the lake property, most of our millworkers came from there.

We got lots of help from our friends at Mount Currie. Charlie Mack Seymour had been a logger and boom man in the Queen

132

Charlotte Islands during the 1920s. He taught me the fine points of axe work and how to move huge logs without machines, by levering them. Charlie was a Saturday night regular at the Pemberton Hotel, always wearing his logger's hard hat.

I recall Ralph Dan and Harry Dick among our mill employees later. One good friend was Dixie Joe, who took daily driving lessons from Carol. Dixie personified the best characteristics of the human race. He and his wife Winnie took in many foster children.

*Charlie Mack Seymour willingly shared his great knowledge of wood and axe-work and his unique skill in moving and placing large logs.*
*Photo Credit: British Columbia Archives*

Our family began to enjoy the lake, fresh air, wildlife, fishing and boating. We experienced the occasional visit by government people checking up on us. Federal Fisheries people made sure we weren't obstructing the sockeye run and B.C. Lands and Forests at Pemberton was worried that we might set the woods afire. We were new to the officials and looked upon as tourists.

But expenses were mounting. We had to find a better solution for transportation.

Horses were not practical; a two-wheel drive car would not make the steep hills. I was on the lookout for an affordable four-wheel drive vehicle that I could leave at the rail station. I soon found this to be out of our financial reach. "When one door closes, another door opens," my grandfather would tell me. So I looked for the open door. It was only open a bit and I had to open it the rest of the way.

## A Whole New Life

At the time, Jim Spilsbury and his lawyer Esmond Lando were partners in Western Isetta Motors. Remember those cute little vehicles made in Europe? Jim signed up for 200 of them, 100 now and 100 later. It had an Italian-made 18-hp motor, two rear wheels close together, two wheels wider apart in front, one seat, the front door opened the full width of the vehicle with steering wheel attached. The idea that this would be a useful vehicle for low-cost transportation in Vancouver was not unreasonable, but it didn't sell.

The 200-car Isetta dealership on Denman Street was going nowhere. It needed sales direction and customers. The innovative little car was just not being accepted. So I cut a deal: one Isetta as a prepayment and I would direct the sales force two evenings a week for six months.

For the sum of $8.50, I shipped the Isetta to Pemberton by rail express. It was so small and light, you could push it onto the railcar by hand. The people around the station in Pemberton laughed and Roy Penrose called it Potvin's popcorn prize; but we had the last laugh.

We loaded our baggage on the two roof racks; Bruce across the backseat, three of us in the front seat with an outboard motor between our legs, and off we went. It was a bumpy ride but we made it. A lot of fun. Later, Bob Taylor, feeling sure disaster awaited us, drove down the lake and was astonished to find us on site enjoying ourselves. He hadn't believed the little car could make it down the lake

It was during summer holidays, a Sunday afternoon, and time for me to catch the train back to Vancouver. We had no assurance the 18-hp Isetta would make it back out. My wife and kids followed my progress by boat, cheering as I made each steep hill. The test came at the final, long, steep hill. I pushed the accelerator pedal to the floor and took off with a burst of speed. Trouble came when I neared the top of the hill.

Because the rear wheelbase was so much narrower than the front, the wheels between them found every bump or hole in the road and there was no way to steer around them. At that point, dips in the road made me lose momentum. I made it the rest of the way by bunny-hopping the car along; clutch in, brake on, rev up the motor, release clutch and brake and leap a few feet ahead. Great clouds of dust began clogging the air cleaner.

135

I arrived at the head of the lake to more cheers from the boat. Once was enough. I would not try it again. I finished the summer driving the Isetta to the head of the lake and getting picked up by boat around midnight. It was so dark, we had trouble finding our camp. We soon learned to leave a fire burning.

At summer's end, I spent another $8.50 and shipped the Isetta back to Vancouver. Fortunately, Sherwood Motors in Vancouver made an even trade for a four-wheel-drive, four-cylinder Jeep station wagon that had seen better days. After checking over this rickety vehicle, it was loaded on a rail flat car. The family was all excited. We now had a vehicle that could navigate the formidable lake road.

In November 1958, Jim Spilsbury and his young daughter Marie accompanied me to the lake on a three-day weekend. Jim, a talented artist (not yet appreciated) painted a beautiful fall scene in watercolours.

The temperature was below freezing. To keep his colours

from freezing, Jim added a little gin to the mix and a little to our glasses as well. This beautiful original painting still hangs in our hall entrance at the lake.

Our enthusiasm for the old jeep was short-lived. The long climb up Joffre Hill in low range allowed the oil in the oil pan to drain backwards, depriving the front crankshaft bearings of oil. This did not come to light until sometime later. The jeep was towed to the rail flat car and shipped to Sherwood Motors in Vancouver. "You need new crankshaft bearings, you must have run low on oil," the mechanic told us.

"Okay," we said, "do the repairs and fix a number of other things too."

During winter in Vancouver, I installed carpeting in the old jeep, painted the body, put on new tires, and generally fixed it up for the tasks it had to do. I drove it in the city snow when most cars couldn't get around. Come spring, it was once again off to Pemberton by rail flat car. Unloaded by now approving locals, we made the first of many trips down the lake, but come May, the same thing happened again, oil flowed back in the oil pan and a knock developed as bearings starved for oil.

A former army mechanic in Pemberton said, "We had the same trouble in France with these jeep engines; they have no oil pump, and for use on long hills we welded baffles inside the oil pan to retard the full flow of oil to the rear of the pan." I took this up with Sherwood Motors. After an embarrass-

*Jean, Heather and Bruce in March 1959. Proudly posing with our first 4-wheel drive vehicle, a ten year old Jeep station wagon.*

ing moment, the salesman, an ex-mechanic and his dad, brave as hell, undertook to drive to Lillooet Lake in a company jeep with a winch to do temporary repairs on the jeep and bring both vehicles back to Vancouver. This was at their company's expense.

The trip took courage. Blacktop to Britannia, winding gravel road to Squamish, Hydro tower access road to Alta Lake (now Whistler). Continuing on the very precarious trip, the adventurers crossed creeks where there were no bridges, found their way through the maze of rocks and logging roads to Pemberton, down and over the hills to Lillooet Lake, to sleep in our trailer, make the temporary repairs and return to Vancouver. The trip would have been impossible if the other jeep hadn't had the winch. Lillooet Lake to Vancouver in 17 hours.

The Sherwood Motor people soon understood the oil pan problem. We made a mutually acceptable deal, trading in the four-cylinder jeep for a brand new six-cylinder Wyllis station wagon. What this vehicle did for us was marvellous, a testimonial to good car design, one that worked, one that you could repair in the bush, not like the computerized four-wheel-drive vehicles people now have to drive to the ski slopes. Lord help you if you break down in some remote area.

## First a Cabin, then a Home

Our dream was for a real home on the lake. We learned that if we paid back the government portion of our soldier's settlement, we could have a $7,500 loan for 10 years at 3.5-per-cent interest. Also, once we built, we could obtain a few thousand dollars more at five-per-cent interest. The VLA (Veterans Land Act) councillor visited the lake, liked it and felt it had potential as a fishing camp, if a road ever came through, and that we might sell off a few lots in the future. Our past service in the air force seemed to help with our application. VLA asked that we parcel off a section of the 128 acres, so we parcelled off 13 acres. The Department of Highways, which approved all rural subdividing, would not approve the partition; the reason given being no legal access existed, meaning no proper highway.

VLA pitched in to help, but only after we complained the

*The beginnings of our 'Panabode' cabin which looked across the lake to a magnificent snowy peak. It took years to complete and it was still far from finished when we moved in permanently in 1966.*

highways approving officer was depriving veterans of their rights. We were down in spirits for a while, but bounced back hearing the good news. The condition the VLA set was: borrow the money from the bank, and when the construction had progressed, the bathroom and kitchen were functional, funds would be dispersed.

We quickly ordered a 1,500-square-foot Panabode 6" cedar log house. Three box cars full of building material, asphalt roofing and 200 bags of cement were shipped up to a rail siding some 13 miles away. I constructed a two-wheel trailer with long tow bar and shipped it to Pemberton in anticipation of the haul down the lake. It was early 1961, during mud season.

Three weeks was all the time I had to haul the materials to the lake site. The local trucker couldn't do the job, because Joffre Hill was too steep for him to climb on the way back to Mount Currie. Following my grandfather Napoleon's advice, "when you want a job done, do it yourself," I made two trips a day, sometimes three, from 6 a.m. to midnight, unloading the midnight trip the next morning.

Unloading the box cars all alone was a feat in itself and back-breaking for a sales type like me. The passenger seats were removed from the new vehicle. The trailer was loaded with pre-machined cedar logs, some roofing went in the station wagon, with three bags of cement on the passenger's front side, one bag of cement on each side of the front bumper and off I went, stopping frequently to adjust the chains on the trailer. Each trip I would add one more bag of cement until I determined the maximum load that could be carried. The jeep, in low, low gear, barely moved on the steep hills. From the beginning, we had named one hill Trouble Hill.

Fortunately for me, the jeep held together. Everything could have been lost and me with it. The 22-foot beams were a real challenge. Loaded level, the beams protruded so far off the rear of the two-wheel trailer that the ends were scraping along the road as I travelled down the wavy jeep trail. To avoid grinding the beams to a point, I nailed scrap wood on the end and replaced it regularly

In three weeks the job was done. Jean had hot meals and quick lunches ready, a warm cozy cabin and clean clothes on hand. I would not have had sufficient strength to load and transport three full boxcar loads alone. Jean helped me unload most trips. We became skilled at cantilevering beams, flipping over asphalt bundles and bags of cement. When we were done, we covered the materials for winter, feeling secure. Knowing the sternwheelers had been out of action for 97 years, there would be little chance of theft.

The locals had watched the city slicker doing his own hauling. I began to earn a small grain of respect in the community. George Walker, a local logging operator, said to me, "I didn't think you could haul it alone."

### Six Years Later...

Our dream VLA house continued to take shape until the money ran out. Then for three years it was only used seasonally, because Cuba called for my full attention. When funds could be found, we installed doors, windows, lino, and we were exuberant to see the house nearing completion. Inside, the scent of cedar was pleasing and the view breathtaking.

In late 1966, we moved up to the lake and decided I would take 1967 off from city work. Bruce and I cut several loads of Christmas trees from under the power line and set up a tree lot near our Point Grey home. It was hard work and a good introduction to business for Bruce.

One day Bruce came home with wild mink in the boat. This led to our mink ranching days. Mink ranching was an episode like no other, but we gave it up when we decided to

142

subdivide the land. Eventually we did this, and it changed my life all over again.

Jean's sporadic alcoholism was creating problems. We could not find effective medical treatment for Jean; she was full of anxiety and frightened, but there seemed to be no one willing to help.

*An afternoon's catch of Dolly Varden and Cutthroat trout at the Narrows at the lower end of the lake. Al Tyson (to the right) built one of the first cabins on the lake below Twin One Creek.*

Jean just loved fishing; most days she caught fish. Living at the lake seemed to abate her illness. I felt whatever demons were inside her, were now under control. Then, without warning, Jean, my wife of 30 years, died. This was a tough blow and it gave cause to reflect on the passage of time.

My enthusiasm for the lake remained, but after 30 years of marriage, to lose your companion suddenly, is a difficult adjustment. Bruce worked at the local mill and on construction of the Duffy Lake road, and he was living with me at the time. With one more boarder I kept busy shopping, cooking, cleaning and washing, appreciating, as they say,

143

what it is like to walk in another person's shoes.

## Out in the Cold

Our radio telephone was the only one in the area. We became the emergency centre for those in distress. Broken-down vehicles, accidents, lost hikers and planes caught in bad weather all brought people-in-trouble to our door. Many had walked miles to reach us and our radiophone.

Nineteen sixty-seven was the only year the lake froze over in the whole time we have been here. I was awakened in the morning by two excited dogs far out on the unfamiliar ice. It was during Christmas holidays and our two teenagers were determined to get back outside for a big New Year's party coming up. The road had just disappeared under a record snowfall and the lake was frozen, but the party was paramount to them.

I walked a short distance out on the lake and axed through the ice to judge its thickness. Under my feet it was about three inches, but it seemed thinner ahead. I came back to the float and tried the boat motor. As I throttled the motor, the boat jumped up on the ice, propeller in the water, the boat folding down the ice as our impromptu ice-breaker travelled along.

The eager party-goers jumped in, suitcases and all, and off we went. It had been arranged for Bruce's friend Brent Pipe to pick up the kids at the head of the lake. They clambered out to wait for him as weather conditions pushed me to return home, breaking and cutting a new trail back. But Brent didn't arrive, because his vehicle had slid off the icy road from Pemberton.

The below-zero temperature and cold wind stirred up panic in Bruce and Heather as they waited. Bruce ran up the road to Nick and Rose Andrew's. Rose massaged Bruce's arms but could not undo the freezing in his hands. Heather, left behind with frozen fingers and hands, waited. Finally Brent arrived, rushed towards Pemberton with his frozen friends, only to slide off the road again, throwing Bruce and Heather out into freezing temperatures.

They finally made it to Pemberton, and

ROUTE TO CARIBOO.

HURRAH

For Cariboo!!

DOUGLAS

AND

LILLOOET ROUTE

IS BY FAR THE

Shortest and Best

BOTH FOR

MEN AND ANIMALS

TO THE

CARIBOO MINES,

As will be seen at once by the following TABLE of DISTANCES, which have been CHAINED by Government, NOT GUESSED AT, as on the Lytton Mule Trail:—

FROM DOUGLAS TO HANCOCK'S 4 Miles.
Thence to Perry's ............. 6 "
    " Hensley's ............. 3 "
    " Chapall's ............. 3 "
    " Gowen's ............. 2 "
    " Stein's (Hot Springs)... 5 "
    " Joire's ............. 1 "
    " Williams' ............. 4 "
    " Pemberton, over the Lillooet
        Lakes now connected by
        Steamer:—Fare, $1.....30 "
    " Half-Way House..........12 "
    " Anderson Lake..........12 "
From Anderson and Seaton Lakes to
    Port Seaton—Fare, $1 to
        each Lake..............34½ "
Thence to Lillooet Flat...........3¾ "
Whole Distance from Douglas to Lillooet by Land over a Good
    Wagon Road..............55½ "

☞ Remember that Lillooet is 45 Miles above Lytton. ☜

On the Lillooet Lake

Goulding's New and Splendid Steamer

"Prince of Wales"

100 TONS BURTHEN,

Will Make Two Trips per Day,

And is capable of taking on board

The Heaviest Wagons

OR

AN ENTIRE MULE TRAIN!

On Seaton Lake

Taylor & Co. are just Completing a
A SIDE-WHEEL STEAMER, THE

*The Sternwheeler "Prince of Wales" that plied Lillooet Lake waters carrying fortune seekers on the first Gold Rush Trail to the Cariboo via Harrison, Lillooet, Anderson and Seton Lakes. The 100-ton Prince of Wales could accommodate an entire mule train or the heaviest wagons. The fare was $1.00 for the twenty mile trip from the Mile 29 stopping house to Port Pemberton at the head of the lake*
*Photo Credit: British Columba Archives*

District Health Nurse Leone Cosulich, summoned from home, gave emergency treatment and put the patients on the train for Vancouver. They were admitted to St. Paul's Hospital, where they stayed a week, recovering from their adventure.

New Year's and the party came and went without them. We have never again experienced so severe a winter and hope we never will.

# CHAPTER 7
# CUBA

Looking back, I find it hard to believe all the things I accomplished in Cuba.

I first became interested in it in November 1959, when I was constructing a cabin by the shore of Lillooet Lake. Jean and I were enjoying rum and coke, the popular drink of the day. Since it was below freezing we had a ready supply of icicles to keep our drinks tinkling. Keeping me company while I hammered and sawed by hand, was the radio tuned to CKDA Victoria, our only station, which was reporting on the advances of Fidel Castro in Cuba.

Six years earlier, I had been to South America on a sales trip. On return, my flight was diverted to Cuba for a scrutiny of passengers. I didn't understand then what it was about, but I knew the Cubans meant business because of the way we were lined up by armed personnel. Cuba intrigued

*Cuban fishing vessels under construction near Varadero Beach outside Havana. We supplied all the communications equipment for the fleet of 125 boats.*

me, as did all Latin American affairs. It was impossible then to know that in three years' time I would be in Cuba, that Cuba would be playing an important part in my life, and most of all, that the business I would generate there would be a major salvation of Spilsbury & Tindall Ltd.

I made business trips there regularly for three and a half years, working under difficult conditions. I learned to deal with the followers of the ideals of Fidel Castro's revolutionary government and with those who did not share a *systema socialista.*

I met Castro himself, and Che Guevara too. I got caught up with the excitement of the moment, the building of so many fishing boats, the experimental farms in the countryside, the fervent attempts to increase the food supply. All this activity in the midst of closed-up shops, transportation failures, empty marinas and cattle on the abandoned golf course.

Working on my own in order to distance the company in Vancouver from the embargoes on trading with communism at the height of the Cold War, I managed to make sales of radio-electronic equipment of more than $1 million – close to $12 million in today's money.

But it was fraught with tensions and business concerns that brought changes in my relations with Spilsbury & Tindall, the firm that I had worked so hard to make prosper.

It all started during the 1950s when we decided to split the Spilsbury & Tindall operation into two companies – manufacturing and sales. This allowed the radio factory to concentrate on manufacturing and the sales company to expand its marketing by offering other products as well. The factory manufactured medium- and high-frequency radio-phones for land and marine use. These products were complemented by those of other manufacturers, such as radar, VHF radios and depth sounders.

With the Canadian market well covered, I, as managing director, had time to concentrate on world markets. I had been to South America in 1953 and my appointment to the first federal Canadian electronics trade mission to Latin America in 1962 just whetted my appetite for more.

Our company received a letter from what was then the Department of Trade & Commerce in Ottawa, inviting me to be a member of a seven-man electronic trade mission to South America with all expenses paid. The letter was signed by George Hees, the minister responsible. I was on holiday at the lake and my assistant mailed a copy to me. My first reaction was not to participate, as we really needed immediate sales. My wife Jean, helping me install windows in our lake chalet, said I should go, it would be a wonderful opportunity.

Later, while on the mission, one member, an engineer with the ministry, informed me that Jim Spilsbury, our company president, had phoned Ottawa and lobbied for his appointment instead of mine, and was informed a very careful selection of appointees had been made and that, if Louis Potvin did not participate, another firm would be selected.

My job on the mission was to represent small electronic companies in Western Canada and our own firm too. At that time, electronic manufacturing was in its infancy in the West. This was the first electronic mission and Ottawa was taking care it be well run. So I went to a briefing in Ottawa, returned to Vancouver and later joined the group in Toronto before we went off to Mexico City, Caracas, Bogota, Quito, Lima, Santiago, Buenos Aires, San Paulo, Rio and New York.

I had been to Venezuela, Colombia, Ecuador and Peru on my 1953 sales trip. I was selling radio equipment on the heels of the sale of seven Anson aircraft from Queen Charlotte Airlines to Ecuador.

While visiting so many centres and markets, I soon realized that if a market could be found with minimal U.S. participation, Canadian products would do better.

Spilsbury & Tindall equipment commanded a diminishing market in Canada, because there was a declining need for medium- and high-frequency communications, as users slowly converted to microwave and very high frequency. The high-frequency bands were becoming congested and the licensing authority encouraged new systems to utilize the very high frequencies (VHF). The use of repeater stations greatly extended the VHF range. Point-to-point microwave towers ensured round-the-clock communication. The market niche for Spilsbury & Tindall equipment was for frontier communication. These frontier areas were more and more accessible, so the need for this equipment diminished, except for isolated pockets where our equipment would be the sole means of communication.

Our high-frequency equipment was extensively used along the B.C. coast, the oil fields, by fishing and towing vessels, forestry departments coast to coast, Hydro projects, telephone companies, the RCMP, small airlines and in Canada's northern areas.

Serving a shrinking market meant I had to be constantly

developing orders farther and farther afield. All of this created a strain on me. Like others, I had a family to look after and was concerned about my options for the future. I had received some very generous offers to move to the U.S. and market other product lines but I could not bring myself to leave Canada. Also, the company, of which I was a minor shareholder and managing director, was very generous to me and I enjoyed job satisfaction at that time.

## *Why Not Cuba?*

In my travels through South America with the 1962 trade mission, Cuba was suggested to me privately as a possible market. I was told that if I went to Cuba, I would go on my own, as there was no trade office in the Havana Embassy. The missile crisis had just passed and there were lingering misgivings about the direction Cuba was taking.

Some said, "You will be killed if you go to Cuba;" others that I would find myself in prison. Still others felt it was only a matter of time before the U.S. would invade the country.

In Ottawa in May 1963, I looked into the matter further and was invited to a Cuban embassy reception which was attended by all East Bloc attachés, some in military uniform, the women beautifully dressed, furs and all. My first introduction to the communist camp.

I was encouraged to go to Cuba by the Cuban ambassador. He would telex Havana and I would be given protocol treatment on arrival. It was made clear to me that numerous contracts would be possible if I could supply the right equipment and trade fairly.

Returning to the factory in Vancouver, I reported on my visit to the Cuban Embassy. Jim Spilsbury and I both being adventurous, we decided it was worth exploring. I was asked to make it a quick trip, as my absence would be felt.

Cuba was accessible only via Mexico City, travelling there by Canadian Pacific Airlines and connecting with Cubana de Aviacion, which had a weekly schedule but never was on time because the run was subject to aircraft being available after Cubana flew its route from Gander, Canada, to Prague, Czechoslovakia.

I felt apprehensive while in Mexico City, awaiting daily a call that the Cubana de Aviacion plane was on its way. Finally the call came. I was told to go to the airport at 11 a.m.

It was not that I was unaccustomed to Latin American countries, as I had been in nearly all of them by now. But Fidel Castro's Cuba was in the communist camp, and all the unfavourable stories about it did give me some concern. To add to the apprehension, all incoming and outgoing passengers were quarantined at the Mexico City airport.

I looked over my fellow passengers and saw several tough-looking guys. I struck up a conversation, but found them not too communicative. I did establish that they were from Bolivia and word was that they were going to Cuba to farm. That may have been true but they did not look like farmers.

The Mexican immigration officer took individual mug shots of each of us and we were locked up in a special departure room for several hours before boarding our flight. The only North American access to Cuba was through Mexico City which permitted the CIA to keep tabs on the comings and goings.

## A Gentleman with a Hole in his Shoe

We finally reached Havana after what seemed an endless night flight, and I was waved through Customs at Jose Marti Airport. Cuban External Affairs had a car and driver waiting for me. The car was an old, expensive sedan that had seen better days. The driver was an articulate man, though dressed shabbily. His black trousers were shiny from wear, and his toes showed through one shoe.

He apologized for his appearance and said this was the best they could do because of the American embargo.

I remember, on arriving that first night, it was hot and humid, the airport people comfortable in white short-sleeved shirts. The tropical heat made you feel it was party time, not like most South American capitals which are located at higher altitudes.

The People's Militia were at all entrances and very friendly. My first impression of Cubans was pleasant and welcoming.

The drive to the Hotel Riviera in the early hours of the morning was not unlike going into any other city, except there were few lights and only one message on the billboards, all about Fidel and the revolution: many signs featuring Castro would read, "Todo Con Fidel" (everyone for Fidel). Other signs would read, "Patria o muerte venciermos" (until death for the Fatherland). The U.S.S.R. hammer and sickle flew alongside the Cuban flag as did, in some places, the stars and stripes.

I was awakened early after a short sleep by the crowing of roosters. The rural people of Cuba had been moved into the city to fill the apartments left vacant after the revolution and lots of them kept chickens on the flat rooftops. It sounded strange to hear barnyard sounds in the middle of Havana. There were also drumming and musical sounds during the night, and I couldn't figure out where they were coming from until finally realized it was from truckloads of soldiers who were beating African-Cuban rhythms on empty fuel drums as a convoy rolled along.

The lobby of the Hotel Riviera featured a very large cardboard placard of Camilo Cienfuegos, a fellow revolutionary with Castro who reached Havana ahead of Fidel and later disappeared.

Cienfuegos was pictured as a hero of the fatherland who sacrificed everything. He too had a long beard that rivalled Fidel's. It was rumoured that Cienfuegos, who had a different philosophy, had to be pushed aside. Leaving the spotlight to Fidel, he was never to be seen or heard of again.

The Hotel Riviera was threadbare. The Americans had taken the hotel plans when they left. The water and electric systems failed frequently. Water was wheeled up to the occupied floors to quench the odour from the overflowing toilets. The air conditioning system was not working and the stench in the hot, humid hallways was overpowering. These hardships served to bring the hotel guests and staff closer together.

The few hotel staff remaining liked having a Canadian in their midst and talking about the old days. I was shown the empty casino rooms, very guardedly, I must say. They couldn't relate to the few Russians they saw. The tension was such that you could feel it. Fear prevailed even among some revolutionaries. Most of them had a member of the family, sister, brother, wife or parents who had left Cuba.

*Cuban government officials on the shipbuilding site,*
*Louis Potvin on the right.*

156

Later that first afternoon, two burly and friendly Cubans arrived at my hotel suite, sporting large revolvers under their belts.

One of these guys had been a member of Fidel's bodyguard, the other active in the revolution, seizing all the boats and yachts that hadn't left Havana. It soon became clear to me this was the welcoming committee who had come to size up this new visitor and decide if he were businessman, CIA, or both.

Before the revolution, Eduardo Puente, the ex-bodyguard, had been an RCA microwave technician who maintained the telephone link with the U.S. The other fellow, Raul Gomez, had been a fishing guide, so I guess he knew the yacht club well. Both had spent time in the States. Gomez had since spent a year in Leningrad training at a Russian university, was now with Cubana de Aviacion and held a rank in the military. After an evening visiting dreary night spots, I was asked what they could do to facilitate my visit to Cuba. I felt I was making progress.

I informed them I needed a guide to facilitate calls I wanted to make, one who knew his way around the government offices. Cuban sales agents were no longer in existence. The few who had been tolerated for a time were so unreliable and dishonest that agents of any kind were frowned upon.

Finally, I was introduced to Rolando Peon who had worked in his family business before the revolution when the family rice mills were seized and nationalized. One of Peon's cousins was imprisoned for smuggling small arms from Spain aboard Iberia flights with the aim of overthrowing Castro. He was caught arriving at the airport with grenades and small arms strapped to his legs. Rolando stayed behind to be supportive of his elderly parents and be near the cousin who was serving a 30-year sentence. He was part of a group that at first helped Fidel, but when they saw what the revolution brought, they became counter-revolutionists.

Rolando told me the cousin had learned five languages while in jail. On my many trips over a three-year period, Rolando had me bring large cartons of powdered milk for his jailed cousin. This was one of the delicate roles I had to play.

Rolando spoke English fluently and looked like the late Desi Arnez, the Cuban-turned-American actor who was then starring with Lucille Ball in the TV hit I Love Lucy. We got along well. At times I wondered what other activities he was involved in.

A deal was struck with the Cuban interior department; Peon could work with me, we would pay him one-per-cent commission which he would turn over to the Cuban government and then in turn receive a much lesser payment of around 100 pesos a month. The Cuban exchange rate was one peso to $1 U.S. but on the black market, a U.S. dollar would fetch anywhere from 3 to 12 pesos depending on the level at which the exchange took place. We all kept a straight face throughout these discussions.

## A Two-way Street

A high-ranking representative of Cuban External Affairs visited me at the hotel on my fourth day.

It appeared Carlos Farias was also there to size me up. Cuba had been fleeced by crooks, so they were discreetly screening me from all directions, both in Cuba and back in Canada, where some agency even went so far as knocking on my neighbours' doors.

But this official was also anxious to pick up hard-to-obtain items for himself and his young wife. He was an elderly man and told me that he felt out of place in the government, as it was a young man's revolution. Before the revolution, he had been a sales rep for American products, and one of his big sellers during the days of gambling in the casinos was Alka Seltzer.

Farias agreed with Fidel that the Americans had corrupted Cuba with gambling and prostitution, and that the cancer had to be eradicated. Now a Marxist and believer in the world socialist order, he chose to stay behind when his wife departed for the U.S. with their daughter.

As the revolution spread across Cuba, many fled Havana

by yacht or plane, for fear of being associated with the Batista regime that was overthrown by Castro. Others took their money and ran to board passenger vessels anchored in the harbour before Castro sealed it. Some assembled makeshift rafts and braved the high seas for the Florida Keys, and some drowned in the attempt.

Later the port was closed tight and nobody got out, except after screening and long delays.

The revolution created havoc among the people. Some were for it and others against. It split families, turned brother and sister against one another.

Say the brother had a small business, a bakery, repair service or the like. It was done away with because free enterprise was not permitted. Say the sister had clerical skills and was recruited in a ministry, maybe one in charge of confiscation. Then the sparks would fly.

I met an engineer whose sister was given a ten-year sentence for counter-revolutionary activities. He could have gone back to the U.S. where he had worked, but chose to devote himself to the revolution to be near his sister, help her and hope to secure her future release by being a devoted companero.

The sense of caution was everywhere. You could feel it when people looked at you, sizing you up and trying to decide if you were good news or bad news.

But many Cubans of mixed blood were rapidly elevated in office after the revolution, and these people were more

160

sure of themselves, more relaxed and fun-loving. Life in the U.S. held no promise for them, only riding in the back of the bus.

Farias told me some hair-raising tales about illicit traders and the trouble they got into (I have a whole chapter on this) and I assured him I would not repeat their mistakes, after which he asked me for more razor blades. I took great pains to cultivate a reputation of reliability and to avoid getting mixed up in any embarrassing activities.

## Learning the Ropes

I visited Farias and his new bride after hours, and we had some dinners together. I remember there was little choice on the menus and the conversation was mostly about the world socialistic order that was evolving. He took great pains to explain to me Cuba needed the help of capitalistic countries only at the moment. Then in the same breath, he asked for bobby pins, curlers and zippers for his young wife.

He said to drop by his office one day and I, believing it was a genuine invitation, took him up on it. My guide and I nodded at the guards to the ministry building with me identifying myself as "Canadiense."

We reported to the reception desk, which was guarded by armed militia, and were shown the stairway and told the room number. We marched down the hall and suddenly, through the open door, we saw Farias seated at his desk,

*Cuba 1995. We visited with a former company technician who was one of the early electronic graduates of Vancouver Vocational School sent by us to Cuba to facilitate on-site work. He married a Cuban girl and remained in Havana to work and raise his family.*

cutting out clippings from Canadian papers and magazines. There must have been U.S. publications too, as the piles were high.

Upon seeing us, he became flustered. He rushed to the door and closed it and said: "You can't come in here. Just how did you get by security?"

He walked us down to the saloon, a grand old reception

hall with a beautiful high ceiling. Spanish-style murals showing former presidents and revolutionaries. He said he couldn't be seen here with us, and for us to leave at once. So we left.

I found fear prevailed in many an office, as people were afraid of being branded counter-revolutionaries by association.

But he must have felt comfortable, no harm done, because following this incident he invited me to dine at a better place, the Rooftop Government VIP Restaurant Lounge, and at Cuba's expense.

Only the most important people were wined and dined in this place. I never saw anything like it in Cuba again. It obviously was left over from capitalist days and was now maintained to entertain those most important to the revolution.

We were served graciously by white-gloved black Cuban waiters, who presented food not seen on the open market. Prawns, shrimp cocktails, filet mignon, mouth-watering dessert. And what a view of Havana!

The Rooftop meal was a big contrast to the times Farias would visit me at the hotel and ask apologetically if I had any toothpaste to spare.

When he did this, I would squeeze some toothpaste into a little container he had ready and give him some blades. I apologized in turn for not being more generous, but explained that I was getting short because the hotel staff squeezed my tooth paste tube daily, and took razor blades from each package.

One of the culprits was the man who cleaned up my room and made the bed. He told me he had owned a huge apartment complex I could see out my window, but it was confiscated and filled with people from the countryside who did not know how to keep the place up. "They even have chickens," he said. "Look at me now – I'm a chambermaid."

## *Finding Food*

Black market sources provided some basic farm products. One of Fidel's sisters had a weekly delivery route of fresh eggs and farm produce, delivering to many high-ranking officials. She differed with Fidel and needed greater income and this didn't seem to bother her customers.

There was lots of Cuban beer, sold in Coke bottles; lots of ice cream. Fidel promised many flavours of ice cream, a promise lived up to. Cuban Coke was available but the formula was not right. Cuban rum was no match for the real thing.

The Hotel Riviera, where we foreigners usually stayed, had a much better menu than other eating places.

Cuba, now a centralized economy, did not have an all-round flow of foodstuffs. Nearly empty supermarkets, with only a few items on their shelves, might find truckloads of watermelons dumped at their doors one day.

We were shown a menu each day, only to be told what we asked for was not available. After a while, we learned to put the menu down, speak to the waiter by his first name and ask:

*"Mario, what's available today?"*

Some days we enjoyed enormous shrimp cocktails. There were often tasty fish dishes and tasty rolls made from Canadian wheat. Vegetables were served intermittently, but fruit dishes were always available, as was strong, thick Cuban coffee.

Frogs's legs could be had for awhile from a state farm set up with the help of France, and eggs and chicken were available from time to time. It seemed strange at times to be the only person seated in the dining room. The hotel tried to keep up its pre-revolutionary standard with white tablecloths and fine cutlery. It was amusing at times.

## A Regular Commuter

I made 12 trips in all to Cuba over a three-year period, including an exploratory visit and an initial protocol visit. In July of 1963, I took my daughter Heather with me on a sales trip and the following February, I took my wife Jean. In July 1965, Heather went back to Cuba with a young engineer I sent down there and stayed for two months at the home of my Cuban guide, Rolando Peon. She returned in early September and came directly to the lake.

Entering and leaving Cuba so often made me realize how others envied the special status I enjoyed. Once, when leaving Havana, I was given the Cuban newspaper Granma, named after Castro's invasion boat. In it was a cartoon showing Fidel wielding a club and chasing a small figure of President Johnson wearing a suit of stars and stripes. On arrival in Mexico City I had to give up the paper because the Mexicans made sure no such propaganda got into the States. But I picked up an English-language paper with a front-page cartoon showing Johnson's face with a small mosquito biting his nose. The mosquito was Fidel, army hat, beard and all. Some contrast!

With each trip, I became more familiar with my surroundings and the requests for personal items grew longer.

It was difficult to sort out all the impressions I got of Fidel's systema socialista. I saw a field full of large bulldozers and asked what they were all doing there. I was told they were a gift from China – 50 of them in total. But the Cubans didn't like them because they lacked hydraulics and other refinements. Russian-made sugar-cane cutting machinery was unreliable and sat in the fields broken down.

Large and small fishing vessels were being constructed on the beaches at an accelerated rate. It was an exciting time.

Raul Gomez accompanied us whenever we were to visit what was considered a sensitive area. His position opened doors for us. We stayed at the Hotel Nacional in Veradero, then used mostly by the militia.

One day in a marina, Raul asked if I would like to board the "Granma," the old wooden boat Fidel and his compatriots sailed from Central America to land his invading party in 1956. Most of the invaders were killed, but Castro and 11 others escaped to conduct a guerrilla war that toppled the Batista government three years later.

The vessel appeared unkept and still had its gun racks in place and no comforts. It was a sorry bit of history when I first saw it, but 30 years later, when I went back as a tourist, it was a white fibreglassed monument, sleek behind hermetically sealed glass walls.

Cubans outside Havana were more relaxed, very warm and welcoming. The weather was hot which called for frequent drinks. It amazed me to see alcoholism appeared not to be a problem with the amount of consumption that took place. The revolution brought day care centres, medical services, schooling and means of higher education. Housing was ten per cent of your income. These benefits were only available to the privileged before the revolution. It is no wonder Fidel received such widespread support from those on the bottom end of the economic ladder.

I asked what Cuba, a small island country, was going to do in 10 years' time with so many engineers, doctors, sea captains and oceanographers. Raul stated these trained people would be needed in the new order of things. Raul was always well dressed, with an expensive watch, quality sunglasses. He asked me to leave behind my attaché case as he took a liking to it. I obliged.

One day, Raul asked if I would like to meet Fidel, sensing that he was about to appear, as his special motorcycle escort, with automatics ready, had quietly arrived and surrounded the marine works area where we were.

A Jeep then arrived and out stepped Fidel, chatting with the companeros. When Fidel came to where we were, the shipbuilding supervisor introduced me as "Ingeniero Luis Potvin del Canada with muy magnifico radio equipment." Fidel thanked me for helping La Revolucion, assured me there would be lots of business in Cuba, and turned away to continue his rounds. Someone asked if I wished to attend another function where Fidel would be, but I declined. I made it clear I was a businessman and not involved in politics. Each day I could see the market potential getting greater and my enthusiasm was on the rise.

My French-Canadian grandfather had counselled me as a boy, "You have too much, you do not have your eyes larger than your stomach." His sayings stuck with me throughout my life and brought reality to many situations

I met Che Guevara, Castro's lieutenant of the revolution,

much later, during the peak of
negotiating sales orders. I was
concerned that Cuba might
default on payments and
asked for a meeting with
Banco Nacional de Cuba. I
was sitting with the bank and
purchasing officials when in
walked Guevara, who was the presi-
dent of the bank before he vanished to the Congo, and was
killed later fighting with guerrillas in Bolivia.

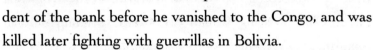

He was imposing and obviously in command. He said I
had no need to be concerned since Cuba could not default
for fear of ruining its credit position in the world market.
The Russians were providing the money but Cuba had to be
solvent.

That said, Che Guevaera stood up and left the meeting.

It was a surprise for me to meet him, since I frequently
walked by his home in Havana but had never caught sight
of him. I can remember seeing his wife rocking on the front
porch of the house and can also remember getting a glimpse
of gun barrels poking through the hedge alongside black soldiers' faces. Needless to say, I looked straight ahead and
kept walking.

Trading with Cuba was quite an experience. I also promoted many orders which our factory could not fill, so we
placed these orders with other small factories.

Canada made excellent electronic products and suppliers were eager to do business, but some small plants in Canada that had parent companies in the U.S. were warned not to do business with Cuba. This didn't seem to bother most suppliers as they were dealing with a Canadian company, Louis Potvin Ltd.

There was some Russian presence in Havana but their activities were kept out of sight of most Cubans. After a while, I could recognize Russians partying at the Tropicana Night Club wearing Cuban dress and speaking only in Spanish. I was warned not to mistake them for Cubans and make some comment I might later regret.

They were ex-Spaniards who went to Russia after the Spanish Civil War, and now the U.S.S.R. was putting them to good use in Cuba. No doubt, some were second generation.

## The World of High Finance

After returning to Vancouver, three trips completed now and still no orders, my enthusiasm was being questioned. When a New York bank was funding our firm's bankers and reviewed the company's financial statement, the unpaid debt was a concern. On the bank's board, at a Montreal meeting, was Frank Griffiths who related to the board the company's prospects in Cuba. This upset the new bankers even more, having had their assets confiscated in Cuba. The bankers wanted to call the loan unless the company ceased pursuing business with Cuba.

I summed it up this way to Jim Spilsbury and the company's lawyer. I felt certain a $505,000 order was on its way and I was sure of more sales for other electronic products. I was so confident of success, I offered a plan where I would resign from Spilsbury & Tindall, remain a director, minor shareholder, set up my own export company, offer right of first refusal to the factory and operate independently. This, I said, would enable the company to distance itself from direct involvement in Cuban sales.

The company's financial situation was acute with no remedy in sight. The shrinking Canadian market and inadequate control on spending were contributing factors. Jim Spilsbury liked the idea of my pursuing my own course of business with the company retaining the right of first refusal. The firm's lawyer,at my expense, incorporated my new export firm and an inter-company agreement was reached. Everyone was happy with the arrangement. In times like these, the only things you can count on is mutual trust, the written agreement really only a guide of expectations.

Later, when the Moscow Norodny bank in London sent a letter of credit in my name for $505,000, an immediate change of attitude took place. This order represented twice the yearly volume the factory was accustomed to producing. Suspicion reared its ugly head and I was accused of being in

171

cahoots with the Spilsbury & Tindall bankers and planning a company takeover. To exacerbate the situation, leading staff members were slipping into my office privately stating they were with me all the way. At first I didn't realize what they were talking about, being so engrossed in the order at hand.

Soon I realized the powerful position I was now in. An unfriendly forceful takeover was never in the cards. Our Cuba business was shaping up like the Spanish Main, the sight of riches disorienting people. When a person's pride is pricked, you can expect to generate unprofessional behaviour. Such was my experience. Comments made to the industry were intended to question my ethics. In the 18 years, history was repeating itself as I had seen it all before, with others being downgraded upon leaving the company or the airline.

The strain being as it was, I terminated my directorship and offered my shares to Jim Spilsbury. I received the exact amount I invested 18 years earlier. When I commented, "Not even three-per-cent interest?", it was said the purchase of shares was a show of confidence, not to make money. It is no wonder today's regulations pertaining to minor shareholders have been stiffened.

The next hurdle came when the factory needed extra financing to process such a large order. Arrangements were made for periodic cash advances. I was on the hook for all this, as was the factory. The relationship improved as delivery of the goods took place.

To ensure smooth sailing, I hired at my expense a young French-Canadian technician for a period of one year to go to Cuba and be on hand during marine installations and help with any problems that might arise. He was a product of an early vocational school training.

Not only did this young man enjoy full payment in Canada, the Cubans gave him a salary in local currency many times the usual rate. I later shipped down a new Valiant car for his needs. A new car in Cuba drew attention and before long he fell in love and married.

My wife Carol and I visited him in Havana some 30 years later. We were treated royally, meeting his attractive wife, their electrical engineer son and their daughter who rode her bicycle to work daily at the American delegation. We were told the Valiant was a godsend and had been repaired and rebuilt until it just wouldn't run anymore.

Over the years, Cuba relaxed its attitude toward agents, and now he and his wife were in the swimming pool business, cashing in on the new hotel boom in Cuba. Before the revolution, his wife's family operated a business in glass chandeliers and the like, which was confiscated. Such was life for many Cubans.

My trips to Cuba continued after the reorganization, booking another $500,000 in orders for other Canadian factories. This was not easily accomplished.

Even high up, in what would compare to the attorney-general's office, officials would make friendly overtures and invite visits to their offices. When I did this, it made some people more timid, but others would embrace you even more.

The legal people wanted elements for their electric stoves, appliances like mixmasters. Many of the requests were made apologetically, but I sensed that it could be unhealthy not to be generous. I purchased such goods in dollars and received payment in worthless Cuban pesos.

As the expectations grew, so did my excess baggage on my visits back to Cuba.

In a country where the usual necessities were not available, I had to be very careful when handing out gifts. It took a lot of tact to meet various requests and not embarrass the recipients.

Many Cubans' tastes were rich. Those who had good positions before the revolution still wanted to live well, and asked only for the best – at times, better quality than we had in Canada. Cubans were only 90 miles from Miami by ferry and many were used to all the luxuries.

But the revolution cut through the classes. Those who had wealth before felt the scarcities, while those who had no previous wealth now found a lot of things better.

I remember some strange things when I reflect on the puzzle that was Cuba in those days – and still is, for that matter.

It took great patience to rustle up business in Cuba, and during the three and a half years of my visits, I had lots of time to reflect on how it was going, what I was doing here and what was happening in my life. And here I was in Cuba, living in the best conditions available there at the time, observing other traders getting into trouble because of bad behaviour, embarrassing conduct and poor ethics.

This was a market that bred such people. Cuba created them, Cuba destroyed them at will, or the traders destroyed themselves.

I kept going only because of the prospect of very large orders, enough to keep the factory operating profitably for a year and a half.

I resolved that I would be attentive to the Cubans' needs. I would treat them fairly on quality, price and post-delivery service. After all, this is how clients would be treated in the home market, so when the potential was greater in Cuba, one had to discipline oneself to provide the same service, not deliver, collect and forget.

Well, it all paid off. Radio telephones for 100 large fishing vessels, 50 more for smaller vessels. Radios for the Red Cross (Cruz Rojo). Parts for TV and radio stations, marine radar and electronic items for Mambisa, the Cuban shipping line.

It was hard work, but well worth doing.

It was important to me to amass greater income to complete the second home we were building at Lillooet Lake, which I had come to love dearly. I wanted to move my wife away from her mother, because I thought the friction between them was part of Jean's drinking problem.

I was also trying to save the factory, which was on the brink of receivership. I wanted to put an end to a business where you worked your guts out, but could find yourself out of a job at someone's whim.

## Coming and Going

It was just as difficult for a traveller to get out of Cuba as into it in those days.

One would have thought it would be a straightforward matter, especially in my case, since I had been given VIP treatment the first time in.

But no, you have to understand the pressures on the revolutionary government in processing the applications of the many Cubans wanting to leave legally at a time when others were fleeing by night, risking the ocean voyage to Florida, often in open, overloaded boats or even homemade rafts. And at times being gunned down by Cuban patrol vessels or helicopters.

The revolutionaries refused to help anybody they conceived as enemies of the new regime and there were so few business travellers that there was no system for expediting their exit documents.

So you had to start making arrangements to leave seven to 10 days ahead. First you reserved your plane seat, although there was no assurance the flight would be made on schedule. Then you had to go to an old part of Havana and push past long lineups of very distraught Cubans waiting to be interviewed for an exit permit. You just had to crash the lineup, then still you waited to be called for an interview. You might be told to come back tomorrow or in a couple of days.

Remember, you would not be dealing with one of the educated, but a zealous revolutionary who was attuned to the revolutionary goals and knew how to promote his own interests. He appraised you suspiciously and made you feel your fate was in his hands. There was a lot of questioning, and after he was assured you weren't connected with counter-revolutionaries or too well acquainted with his superiors, he would present a list of his personal requirements. I was asked to bring back spark plugs for an American car, a tire and consumer goods not available like razor blades, etc. I brought them back on my next trip and advised when they could be picked up.

You soon learned that it was good for your health to cooperate. You might see the man again on your next trip out, and you did not want any hassle. But at no time would you get any special treatment. He would be friendlier but still look you over suspiciously. I got the impression these people

177

came from the lowest form of Cuban life, and I hated to be under their control.

You felt some guilt, as well as a sense of importance, to have your passport returned to you when so many Cubans were waiting days in line for exit papers. You felt whole again, to have your passport in your own hands, but you weren't home-free yet. You still needed an entry permit (visa) for Mexico and this meant negotiating another crowd at the Mexican Embassy.

The first time was easy. I walked through the crowd, waved my passport at the Cuban soldier outside the big iron gate, opened the gate and walked in. I showed the Mexican official my passport and exit permit, and received my Mexican entry papers after a money exchange to cover the fee and a bonus to show my appreciation.

A few days later came the actual flight out. I was up at 4 a.m., having arranged the night before for a taxi to get me to the airport by 6 a.m. It was a broken-down relic but the only one I could get.

I was accommodated in a waiting room apart from the exiting Cubans, whose outgoing baggage was checked in detail. The gusanos, the "worms" who didn't support the revolution, were allowed out with only the clothes on their backs, one pen, one watch, a one-time change of under-clothes and no more items of value. Their bags were filled with photographs, rosaries and religious paraphernalia.

I, on the other hand, was escorted out to the plane by

immigration officials and my guide. The initial trip was the only time I got VIP treatment.

"Oh, just a minute Señor Potvin," my guide said as I stepped onto the stairway leading up to the plane. "I forgot. Would you mail these letters in Mexico City for me? The letters are open. You can inspect them if you wish."

I got just a glance from the immigration officer when he wished me a nice trip. I realized when I took the letters that this was a touchy thing to do.

When I was in the air and settled down, I took the package of envelopes out of my breast pocket and looked at them.

I was flabbergasted to see that the letters all contained Cuban passports and were going to addresses in Puerto Rico, Guatemala, Panama and other destinations. Was I now rooked into a passport delivery system?

I wondered who the recipients were and finally decided they must be Cubans who had fled without proper identity and now wanted passports to identify themselves for their new life.

I swore I would avoid being put in this situation again, and the first thing I did on landing was go to the post office, buy Mexican stamps for the letters and put them in the mail.

It didn't get much easier to leave Cuba on subsequent trips, although I made many of them and learned a few short-cuts. Although becoming known to more officials created another problem, referred to as "deep pockets."

Capitalism was gone, the Americans were gone, consumer goods were gone, except for some scarce commodities from Soviet bloc countries. So the business traveller would be asked over and over again to bring back something. And accommodating these requests became very costly!

After the first couple of adventures getting an exit visa, my trips home and back were more or less routine, as the opportunities and the problems were resolved. The black market exchange for U.S. dollars went on from top to bottom. It was against regulations for Cubans to have American dollars in their possession. House searches were conducted but stopped when it was realized the police were keeping some of the money for themselves. After my last departure from Cuba, my devoted guide Rolando fled to the Mexican embassy and was spirited out of the country for reasons unknown to me. I have never seen or heard of him since.

Cuba has now nearly come full circle. It has taken a lesson from the past and kept out gambling, but everything else has returned. Two economies exist, the U.S. dollar market and the worthless Cuban pesos. Civil engineers, doctors and other professionals work at the tourist bars due to lack of opportunity and low income. Freelancers pay the Cuban government a fixed U.S. dollar amount and keep the rest. It can still be unhealthy to exhibit too much wealth as some consumer goods can only be obtained on the black market. Those in the pesos market strive for better times and wonder what happened to Fidel's systema socialista that was to look after them. Cuba is evolving a mix of controlled capitalism and socialism. Does it not remind you of home in some way?

*Hotel Riviera, Havana. All foreign businessmen were required to stay here when in Cuba. I was assigned an eleventh-floor balcony suite facing the harbour. It was luxurious accomodation even though we were often without electricity and water.*

# CHAPTER 8
# THE TRADERS

Cuba was a kaleidoscope of impressions for me, from the hope and despair of the systema socialista, the friendliness of the Cubans when they came to trust you, the schemes of many to leave and the hoarding of U.S. dollars, to the frightening stories of swashbuckling illicit traders and the penalties they paid when they got caught.

My contact at the external affairs ministry, Carlos Farias, told me stories about Canadians who got into trouble trading in Cuba, to warn me, I guess, about what I should avoid.

In the first wave of so-called businessmen after the revolution, he said, was a young Canadian who had a light plane and flew frequently from the Bahamas to Havana. He was taking things back and forth at a time when expensive paintings, French perfumes and jewellery were disappearing from the country. It was said that even Che Guevara had given out paintings in return for foreign goods, such were the shortages in Cuba.

One time, the pilot arrived with boxes full of cans labelled papaya and the customs inspector wondered about the weight of these tins. With so much papaya grown locally why is he bringing in more? So the inspector got a can opener and found grenades in the cans!

Obviously the trader was bringing in contraband for the counter-revolutionaries and getting paid in U.S. dollars. They jailed him for 15 years, then returned him to Canada . Years later, his name was well-known.

Another early trader, who was still operating when I arrived, had previous convictions for smuggling cigarettes into Canada, but the Cubans were desperate for hard goods because of the U.S. embargo. This fellow managed to get luxury cars and motorcycles shipped from the U.S. to Algeria, then back to Cuba.

He obtained for the Cubans items we could not legally export from Canada. World War II export controls were still in effect, although outdated, and everyone recognized it. For example, Cuba needed parts to maintain its RCA microwave telephone link to Florida, but these components were on the strategic list and could not be exported from Canada.

I refused such orders, but some of my sharp colleagues managed to slip through Canadian Export Controls to ship goods.

In contrast, I had export permits to sell Cuba the latest in marine radar, which illustrates how out-of-date the Canadian regulations were.

This trader became so important to the Cuban economy that the government got him a posh rented villa for $100 U.S. a month. The property had belonged to a Cuban lawyer who fled after the revolution. A lot of the furniture had been pilfered, but it was a grand place, with a kidney-shaped swimming pool. Here he housed his beautiful mulatto companion.

## *Thanks, But No Thanks*

The trader heard that I was promoting large sales of radio communications equipment and made overtures for me to team up, but I had been warned to stay away from him. Actually his day was passing, now that Cuba was finding it possible to trade with established people. The Cubans created the monster and had to dispose of him in time because their mutual activities caused such embarrassment. I heard many years later that he had set up business in Saudi Arabia selling tires after the Gulf War.

The third Canadian trader Farias told me about came from a family of tobacco growers in Southern Ontario. He was working in Mexico as a crop expert and was invited to Cuba to help out after a hurricane that had washed salt water over tobacco fields and other crops. He came up with

185

a plan and a $10-million contract was issued for fertilizer and machinery. Fertilizer was a problem, because the U.S. forbade shipment to Cuba, even from U.S. subsidiaries in other countries, but this resourceful fellow bought all he could in Canada and found the balance from other undisclosed sources.

He was given the red-carpet treatment, and instead of being billeted with the rest of us in the foreigners' quarters at the Hotel Riviera, he was given a luxury suite in the Hotel Capri. This splendid hotel was formerly owned by the American movie star George Raft, who had to leave his holdings behind after the revolution.

I met this trader often, but I could see that success had gone to his head. He had a succession of women in to entertain him, and became quarrelsome and rude with the hotel manager.

One morning, when I was leaving Havana for Mexico City, I overheard one of the immigration officers at the airport phoning the Maquimport buying agency.

"If you want him, I will hold him back," the officer said. "When he is gone, he is gone."

I realized they were talking about my trader friend. They took him off for questioning and later jail.

What happened, I was told, was that the Cubans claimed some of the machinery they paid for was incomplete, and they wanted compensation which had not been forthcoming.

I also heard that while he was in jail, the police sergeant became the owner of his car after a repaint job. It seemed if you wanted to eat decently in jail, it called for a payment to the jailers. He was allowed phone calls to make financial arrangements so he could be repatriated to Canada.

This called for some side benefits to the jailers as well. A completely normal state of affairs.

## Making a Deal

But the international political climate affected different people in different ways. Many Canadians felt the U.S. had been unfair towards Cuba. Rarely would a potential supplier ask me to leave his premises.

So two-way trade carried on. The Canadian government and Canadian farmers were glad to see grain sold to the U.S.S.R. and loaded on Russian ships which took it to Cuba. Canada also sold Cuba breeding cattle and pigs, and so many chicks that, from the air, the fields near the Havana airport looked like they were covered in snow.

A Canadian group was flying cargo to Cuba from Toronto on a weekly DC-3 service. That is how the chicks and some cattle arrived. Others arrived by freighter. One night flight was not unloaded on arrival and all the chicks died of the heat.

Quite inadvertently, I got involved in one of the trading adventures. It had been a busy day for me in Havana, call-

187

ing on the purchasing section, Maquimport. Even though a revolution had taken place, the heat and slower Latin pace took their toll. Appointments were hard to obtain and once you got to the purchasing floor, you had to be resourceful and aggressive to see the right buyers.

I noticed one prominent buyer in the hall with a number of people around him. He glanced our way and waved at Rolando, whom he knew well. He handled the purchasing of wire and cables, and Rolando told me he had been with the former Batista government and had finally talked himself into this new post. I liked knowing the background of people I met as it made it easier to communicate. Some were obsessed with Castro, others raging at the evil U.S., and many were longing for better days in the future.

After a long day I went to bed in the hotel. At about 2 a.m. I heard a hard knock on the door.

"Open up," called a voice in Spanish. "It's Ramon, from Maquimport. I saw you with Rolando this morning."

In my pyjamas, I opened the door cautiously and let him in. He came in well soaked in alcohol and asked for a drink of Enejo, old rum. He knew I had Bacardi rum from Mexico, which was smooth as silk, compared to the rum the Cubans were bottling under the Bacardi label.

Ramon sat down, then stood up staggering, and a long-barrelled handgun rolled down inside his pantleg to the floor! He picked it up and I was relieved when he wedged it part way under his belt instead of pointing it at me.

After a couple of Enejos, he was ready to talk business.

188

"You must come see me," he said. "I have prices from Socialist bloc countries but we prefer North American quality if the price is okay."

He added (as I might have expected) that he might have some expenses he would like us to help him with.

We visited his office several days later and he appeared nervous. He said loudly in front of his staff that his preference was with the Soviet bloc sources, but that we should come back again if our prices were right.

I realized that many buyers used this line to reassure other revolutionaries who might be listening of their devotion to the cause. But some brave fellows, feeling more secure, would say:

"The hell with the poor-quality stuff from the Soviet bloc countries. Let's buy from Canada if the quality is better. Look what happened when we bought telephones from Bulgaria!" They were not compatible or reliable.

I found out that people working for the regime were walking a tightrope. Rolando explained that Cubans paid 10 per cent of their salary for housing rent, but your status and connections had a lot to do with the quality of accommodation you got. Health care and education were free. It was good in theory but it was a bare bones existence. One, however, has to admire the gains Cuba made in these fields compared to other Latin American countries.

It was when I returned to Cuba on my next trip three weeks later that I heard about Ramon's plight.

He had amassed $15,000 U.S. for a night-time escape to Florida on a Cuban fishing boat. The captain of the fishboat agreed to bring the boat near an isolated point and for Ramon and his family to come out in a rowboat when he saw a light flash.

When the light blinked, Ramon, his wife and teenage son made their way down a trail to the beach, but suddenly they were caught by a policeman who arrested them and seized the money.

It was a set-up. The fisherman and the police showed their zest for the revolution and were honoured, but they kept most of the money themselves, turning some of it in to the government. Old habits die hard.

This was only one story. There were many the same.

After I heard this, we drove by Ramon's residence, a lower flat in an apartment building, and I was told that only his wife was now at home.

Ramon was sentenced to 10 years at a prison work farm, the 16-year-old son was sent to an indoctrination school and enrolled in the Cuban army. No young people were allowed to leave the fatherland, although Castro encouraged the gusanos to leave the country, as they were a liability.

Ramon's wife could visit him every few weeks, and would tell afterwards of Ramon marching to the work field in military formation, with a shovel over his shoulder instead of a gun.

I do not know the outcome. He may have qualified to leave Cuba after serving his sentence, or he may have died at the work camp.

This was the atmosphere a visiting sales engineer had to work in. You had to discipline yourself not to get involved in politics, just be a reliable trader and bring the orders back to Canada.

*The International Hotel on Varadero Beach. In my time Cuban officials deserving of special reward had government-paid holidays here. Years later, In 1995, the hotel was filled with Canadians from the Toronto Italian Community. A few Cubans were still enjoying the traditional rewards.*

One time I left Cuba with a list of shoes the customs and immigration people wanted for themselves. I bought them in Canada and took them as far as Mexico City on my CPA flight. But I didn't want to carry the 18 boxes while awaiting my Cubana flight, so I asked the Mexican Customs people to hold them. They made a big fuss and would not consider holding them until I showed my appreciation by opening up my billfold.

The flight to Havana was called a few days later and the Mexicans helped me with my boxes. I left them with Cuban Customs when I arrived in Havana about 2 a.m. But I got an angry call from them the next day. They had found that the new shoe boxes contained used shoes with cardboard inserts covering the holes in the soles.

I explained myself to the Customs official and said the exchange must have occurred at the Mexican airport.

"Mexican banditos!" the official exclaimed. "They do this to us all the time."

I guess a smart pair of Canadian shoes was an attractive exchange for a Mexican making $30 a month.

My second trip out was a toughie. I didn't find out why until later. The story was that two "Irish" Canadians had been in Cuba on a holiday, living it up at the black market money exchange and arriving drunk at the Mexican embassy. The officials told them they'd have to come back next day for their Mexican entry permits and their tempers flared. They began shouting and swearing and started to wreck the office until the Mexicans threw them out and locked the gates.

They complained to the Canadian embassy when they sobered up, but it took several hundred dollars to soothe the Mexicans. The pair were finally given visas and told never to come back again.

## Going Out in Style

This happened the week before I asked the Mexicans for a visa and was very firmly refused. So I went to the Canadian embassy for help and was told Canadians were persona non grata at the Mexican embassy since the bust-up.

It became quite a farce. The Canadian attaché phoned the Mexicans and after considerable smooth-talking, they agreed to receive me. But the attaché, worried about my welfare, ordered the embassy black limo out with the uniformed driver, and off we went with the Canadian flag flying on the front fender!

The crowd of Cubans waiting for visas parted as the official car made its way up to the iron gate and the Cuban military guard stepped aside for it appeared to be an official visit.

I was advised to stay calm and polite when I presented my passport. I remember the officials were scowling as they

193

looked at the pages stamped by most Latin American countries, but they looked up as the attaché came in behind me and a very polite exchange took place.

I got the permit, didn't pay anything, was driven away in the embassy car and was at Jose Marti airport at 6 a.m. the next day for my flight to Mexico City.

## Down the Hatch

But I must tell you about the time I got involved in a vodka-drinking contest with the Russians.

A big Aeroflot plane had come in on the maiden flight of service between Moscow and Havana.

The aircraft was so huge, the airport ramp workers had to put a stepladder on the top of the gangway stairs to reach the entrance door.

It was quite an occasion, and the first I saw of the crew was when the captain came into the cocktail lounge of the Hotel Riviera with a flight attendant. He was handsome in his light blue uniform, and the flight attendant was a slim, attractive woman.

We businessmen used to meet in the lounge and everyone was excited about the event so we offered them a round of drinks, but they politely refused, ordered a round for themselves and left.

That was the aircrew. Then we met the ground crew, who were flown out with their wives for the occasion and were quartered temporarily on the 11th floor of the hotel, where I and other foreigners stayed. These people were a different breed.

It was a beehive that night. They left their room doors open while the heavy drinking and visiting went on. I popped my head into one room and a glassful of vodka was thrust into my hand. I sipped at it for a while, then went back to my room and got several boxes of Kleenex as gifts for the wives.

The reaction was strange. They just stared at the boxes, with no sign of appreciation. I guessed they didn't know what Kleenex was for or did not know how to handle a gift from a capitalist.

Then one fellow hauled me into the room, sat me in a chair, poured himself a glass of vodka. He gulped it down in front of me, wiped his mouth with his hand and gestured that it was my turn. I countered with a package of Chiclets, he poured the full box into his mouth and swallowed. I think he thought they were candy.

But now it was my turn to drink, and I took my time, with him watching impatiently. When I managed to finish, while the men and their wives looked on and laughed, he poured himself another and drank it down.

My turn again. Another glassful. I took one sip, said in Spanish that he was the better man and left the room.

Next, I was in the room of an American reporter for Newsweek who was in Havana on a special visitor's permit.

Also there was the Russian correspondent for Pravda, who was fluent in English and Spanish. The three of us were talking over a lighter drink than I'd had in the other room. We were carefully skirting the issues of the day, when in staggered my vodka-drinking friend, smashed out of his mind.

He had a tin of fish, somewhat like herring, and he picked one up by its tail, put his head back and gulped it down like a seagull. Then he insisted I have one too. I tried to imitate his style and dropped one down my throat, but it felt like a garden rake going down and I wanted no more.

He grabbed another fish for himself and fell backwards like a board when he tipped his throat back. He was out cold.

Turns out he was a Bulgarian, not a Russian. "Bulgarians," sneered the Pravda man. "They're nuts."

I have read that power is fortified by destruction and by creation. It is reaffirmed by the very powerlessness of the losers and by the gratitude of those who have gained or believe they have gained. Many of us have difficulty understanding this simple equation while appraising Cuba.

So what is next?

# Chapter 9
# The Mink Ranch

You might ask, "What is a sales executive doing mink farming?"

Well, it was not my intent to be a mink rancher but circumstances were such that it was the appropriate thing to do. I do think my French-Canadian ancestry exerted a magnetic pull on me toward the land.

It was 1966. I had been operating my export company, Louis H. Potvin Ltd., out of Vancouver successfully for some three years, and was now spending more and more time at our Lillooet Lake retreat.

The road to Whistler, no more than a goat trail, had been pushed through and extended to Pemberton. It was a rough gravel road and only the hearty travelled all the way. The steep Hydro access road down Lillooet Lake did not deter us.

We liked it; we liked the escape from Vancouver and its

pressures. The year before, I had toured Vancouver to Montreal with engineers from Cubana de Aviacion, visiting numerous electronic plants, all at my expense. This promotion did not bear fruit, as the Soviets would not fund the technological upgrade, having decided Cubana Airlines should utilize only products from Soviet bloc countries.

The disagreement between Cuba and the U.S. had not gotten any better and I felt that since I had honoured all our Cuban sales commitments, it was time to move on.

The summer of 1966 was time to reflect about what to do now with my life. I had many prospects, but no longer relished being away so much. My wife and I decided I would take a year off, doing nothing but enjoy the lake and fish.

We decided to move to Lillooet Lake with our son Bruce, who would attend school in Pemberton. Our daughter Heather was attending University of B.C., managing our Point Grey home and boarding students, with all the problems that entailed.

In the summer of 1967, the family – all four of us – motored to Montreal to see Expo 67. This was very exciting for us. Jean was brought up in Montreal, and we were married there when we were both in the air force. I had been back several times on sales trips.

Anyway, we adjusted easily to life in our isolated haven. Bruce was an ardent boatman and expert fisherman. One day when he was 15, he came to the dock yelling, "Come see what I've got in the boat."He had been fishing at the mouth of a large creek, he had his catch in the boat and there were mink swimming to the boat, jumping in and hauling the fish away!

When the last one jumped into the boat, the fish were all gone, but Bruce started the motor and sped home with this strange shrieking animal. I got to the dock and figured it must be a mink.

Bruce wanted to keep it for a while, feed it and fatten it up and then let it go as he had done with other wild things, so I agreed. I brought out a new metal garbage can and asked him to throw his jacket over the mink, pick up the bundle and unroll it in the can so I could trap it by putting the lid on.

The shrieks were frightening. I didn't know it then, but this was a 60-per-cent grown kit born in the early spring.

We realized it would need water, air and food. We put a screen over the can, punched holes in the bottom for drainage, added a container of water and dropped in food we thought a mink might eat.

We looked up "mink" in the encyclopedia and other books and found they are raw meat eaters that also eat some vegetation. The raw steak was eaten up, the water consumed and the animal slept quietly in the bottom of the can. I threw in some dry grass so it could bed down.

I looked up mink in the yellow pages and contacted the Co-op food suppliers. The manager, Jim King, said, "You should try and capture more mink and start a ranch strain of wild mink."

He said I should go to Vancouver and they would sell us some feed, cereal and meat wastes that we could keep frozen until needed.

So I went ahead, got the feed and a few discarded pens a rancher gave us. We moved our prize mink into the new pen and he seemed to like it, especially the sunshine he didn't get in the garbage can!

We also came back with a mink-catching box, and in no time at all, Bruce had a whole family of kits trapped along with the mother. He found another family and captured them too. Then, one day on his way home from school, he found a large male mink dozing in the autumn sun on the riverbank.

He caught it with his bare hands, wrapped it in his jacket and brought it home tied to his motorbike. I found out later that he was able to catch it like that because mink are very slow to awake if dozing in the sun.

Bruce, with his few wild mink, had the beginning of a mink ranch and we thought that if we built a mink shed, got pens and purchased some ranch mink for cross-breeding, we might really start something.

## All About Mink

I became more interested and thought a small mink ranch might be a suitable family enterprise at the lake.

This was wishful thinking, based on high profits of earli-

*Feeding mink in October 1970. Each time the feed cart entered the shed a rumble of excitement swept down the row of cages. The card above each cage recorded all pertinent data on the occupant.*

er ranchers who created the Silver Blue mink and other mutations, all to satisfy fashion's whim. All those participating earned considerable profit on the New York fur market.

I visited several mink ranches in the Fraser Valley and read all the books I could find on mink husbandry. I bought several Pastel mink and several old pens, and set them up together with our wild mink: one mink per pen, each pen with a watering cup and feed area where pre-mixed food was scooped in each day.

We built our first mink shed out of local timber, with the help of Charlie Mack Seymour, a Mount Currie neighbour, made our own cedar shakes, and constructed wire pens with aluminum dividers able to accommodate 250 mink. Friends Elmer Chumley – a Pemberton High School math teacher known to everyone as Chum – and his wife Ruth offered welcome help on weekends. Chum helped mostly with building the sheds and Ruth worked on the mink pens.

We later purchased more mink, some Sapphires (Silver Blue) and some Pearls. This was another mistake, as we found it was more profitable to have a large quantity of one colour than a mix of colours.

Breeding was a challenging experience the first year. There are two ways: take the male to the female or take the female to the male. I preferred the latter, but the breeding activity kept me hopping. The procedure is to breed each female twice, with a different male each time, seven to ten days apart.

The last mating will override the first, that is if the male sperm is lively. We did at times have split litters and the colours of the kits would match the parents' records. This was important because you breed for fur quality, size and temperament.

I wore coveralls with a pocket full of clothespegs. The pens with females to be bred that day were identified with one clothespeg. If the pair became coupled, two clothespegs; if mating was consummated, three pegs.

Consummation was tricky. The male mink has a hooked penis, and once they were coupled, they could not be pried apart, even if the male was lifted by his tail, until the male released his hold. But mink seep sperm rather than ejaculate, so we would limit the seeping time to conserve the male's energy for another breeding. As you might imagine, this can make the males angry.

This was a busy time. If everything was lovey-dovey after the mating, there was no rush to separate the pair, but if the male became aggressive and dangerous, I had to rush to take the female out of danger.

After this procedure, the female would be returned to her pen and notations made on her card, which hung from a peg on a clothesline over the pens.

Early March was breeding time, with a gestation period of six to eight weeks. The kits were mostly born from April 24 to May 10, and in June we had a family of mink in each pen.

It was interesting to observe the difference between wild and ranch mink. Wild mink, when placed with a ranch mink, would never fight, and would not breed while I was in sight; nor would they eat if anyone could be seen, but would just pretend they were sleeping.

Ranch mink bred to wild mink produced very large litters. The mix was explosive. A mother could not feed that many, so some were taken away and placed with a mother with a smaller litter, in order to get enough milk. Before placing the kit in the new home, I had to drop it on the manure pile in the pen so it would take on the odour of the new foster family. Some were accepted; others were tossed out.

Notations were made on the cards to give us a history of each mink for the purpose of future breeding for size, quality and behaviour characteristics. You want a strain of contented minks, not ones that leap at your throat when you open the lid of the pen.

## Don't Get too Friendly

If you're mink ranching, you have to avoid looking upon mink as pets. However, you just can't help liking some of them.

There were seven kits born in one of our litters. At first they were all doing well as far as I could see during my daily inspections. Then one day I noticed one kit had a foot missing. The next day his leg was gone up to the knee, and the third day it had vanished up to the end of the upper limb.

This poor little guy was being sucked up bit by bit. Had I not removed him from the litter, his entire innards would have been sucked up by his brothers and sisters.

I placed him, three legs and all, in a separate pen. He couldn't get around to eat or drink, so I placed a piece of cardboard and put water, food and small pieces of liver by his nose.

He soon learned to suck it up and it wasn't long before the wound healed and the hide covered the stump of a leg. He had three perfect legs and would poke the stump out through the hide when he needed it for balance.

The mink became used to being handled and grew up docile. In time, I fed him on top of the cage as he could climb up the wire with three legs and a stump to eat off the top like all the others. This guy had courage.

I put extra liver in his feed, and it showed up in a pinker nose and mouth. He was a healthy specimen with nice fur.

I would tickle his belly at feeding time and I took to leaving the lid open so he could poke his head out and see me working in the aisle. I eventually carried him under my arm as I made the feeding rounds.

I was told by ranchers you can make a pet out of only about one in 5,000 mink. If I had put my finger on another mink, I would have had a tooth sunk through it, which has happened to me. The only way to get the mink to relinquish his hold is to put the curved handle of a set of small pliers down his throat.

We inoculated for distemper (the same type dogs carry) and for virus enteritis, an abdominal infection – both shots at the same time, one in each hind leg. We also gave penicillin shots to those that had developed head boils after a fishbone had pierced and infected their palate.

### He was a Mama's Boy

When raising mink you see many behaviour patterns that seem human.

Once, a Silver Blue mother gave birth to a single kit – a no-no for the profit-and-loss statement. The male kit soon grew to be bigger than his mother, and the two got along so well that there was no need to separate them. The kit never learned to climb the wall to eat off the top because his doting mother brought him all his food.

Here he was, longer than his mother, lying on his back with his fat belly sticking up, and his mother would bring him little bits of food and place them on his chest. His mouth would reach down to eat, and when he couldn't reach it, the mother would nose it closer to his mouth.

This was truly a mama's boy.

I finally had to separate them because the food the mother put on his chest was staining the pelt and I wanted this to stop before his winter fur set in.

It took a couple of days for him to learn to eat like the rest of the mink after his mother was taken away. Mother and son did pine for one another for the first few days.

Once, just after gestation time, a low-flying jet from Air Force Base Comox flew over the lake, breaking the sound barrier and creating panic in the mink shed. New-born kits were eaten by their mothers, bitten, tossed out of the pen or trampled to death, all in one or two minutes.

The sonic boom was so strong, it opened doors in the house and I thought for sure all the windows were broken. I filed a damage claim against the air force and the insurance adjusters settled on the basis of the market value of the pelts of the lost kits. But this wasn't much. I explained that kits are born naked, a pink colour, about one inch long, and the pelt is only marketable after the mink grows winter fur. In time, reasonable financial compensation was made.

Pelts normally prime in late November, the date subject to the length of daylight. Our mink primed early because of the shorter daylight hours in this mountainous area. This led us to approach mink ranching seriously, so we purchased, at considerable expense, 100 females and 20 males. All jet black, from the finest strain of mink in the Fraser Valley.

More mink sheds were built and we concentrated on the jet blacks, phasing out the other colours, except for a few outstanding specimens. We did keep some mink that were offspring of the mixes with wild mink. These kits now behaved just like the others and were happy in their sur-roundings. Our mink sheds were clean, with water running in troughs past each pen end to end of the building. We finally had four sheds, one with six rows of pens 200 feet long, housing 800 mink. We put a plastic pail in each pen to amuse the mink. It was interesting to see all the uses they had for the pail. Bouncing it around with their noses, cover-ing themselves with the pail upside-down, even sleeping in the pail.

## I Needed Help

I was used to wearing suits, travelling, staying in good hotels or being in the midst of activity in the radio plant. I would look up at the snow-capped mountains and out at the emerald-coloured lake, with nobody else around for miles, and wonder what I was doing here, feeding mink and cleaning mink shit.

But I looked at my new world of mink and realized the reason I was doing this was to live in a back-to-nature environment, to try to make it an economic success and to provide a small family business.

I truly believed that, in time, the area would open up with roads and services, and then we could look toward land development, as this was the only privately owned property on the lake. I had decided to make my future living in the area and not go back to the city rat race.

This was not easy to do. I found myself suffering mild depression. In the city, I was used to making lists of things to be done, then assigning those tasks to others. A manager gets a lot done that way.

Now I found myself in the mountains with only the occasional worker, and still making lists. I could not meet my own demands, as listed. So I had to adjust the work list to suit the time frame available. It then seemed that I was not making progress and it was only when I got extra help that my mental state improved.

It was hard to get enough help to do all the chores of a mink ranch, and that led us into a strange encounter.

We got talking to the young Japanese cocktail waiter at the Avalon Hotel in North Vancouver, where we stayed on visits to the city, and he thought it would be a good job for his father, who still lived in Japan.

I thought it might work out because I had been impressed with the industriousness of the Japanese workers on my trade visit to Japan 12 years before. Before I knew it, Hiro had phoned his father in Japan and reported back to me that Papa-san had accepted the job!

I was so bemused by this that I agreed to see Immigration, sponsor the father and pay his airfare. Three months later, I wired the Canadian embassy in Tokyo to ask when he was coming, and I got another lesson in Japanese culture. Turned out he had passed his medical and was ready to leave but I was expected to sponsor his wife as well.

That wasn't the deal but I said okay, and soon they flew to Vancouver, but didn't turn up at the lake. I was learning fast, but not fast enough. I phoned Hiro, who said his parents weren't interested in working in such an isolated place. I spelled out the facts, that they had to get up here at once and start working to pay off the money I spent on their airfare.

It went on like that. We had to meet them at the top of Joffre Hill in the four-wheel-drive because Hiro's car wouldn't make it down to the lake and back. And Mama-san didn't like Canadian food or anything else about the place although Papa-san thought he would be happy here. At least as far as we could tell, as we struggled to communicate with the aid of an English-Japanese dictionary of enormous size.

It came to a head when our pet cat urinated in Mama-san's open suitcase and she demanded a radiophone call to

209

Hiro in Vancouver. We couldn't follow the exchange but Hiro came on the line to say Mama-san was going to Vancouver for a few days, and we were to take her to Pemberton where he would pick her up.

Then Papa-san got a call from Vancouver and reported Mama-san was not coming back but he would stay here on the job. A few days later there was another call from Mama-san and Papa-san started crying, locked himself in his room and would not come out.

We were afraid he might commit hara kiri but finally he came out, sobbing, dressed in his black Japanese suit with brass buttons, all our gifts stacked neatly to be returned, and asking to be returned to Vancouver.

I talked over this failure in cultural exchange with a Japanese United Church minister, who ran a centre for Japanese in transit. He said Hiro was an example of the spoiled younger generation, who probably used us to bring his parents to Canada so he could use their money.

But the minister did find us numerous well-educated and reliable young Japanese men who worked for us for weeks at a time.

As for Hiro, he visited us at the lake with Papa-san several years later to pick mushrooms. And he placed a large order for lumber from our mill, to be exported to Japan. He defaulted on a second lumber order, and we had to send in a trucker to reload it on the dock and deliver it elsewhere where we would be paid.

Now back to mink breeding. You felt like God in a way, deciding who bred whom. You could see how the idea of creating a master race came about. Granddads were bred to granddaughters, so as to pass the best characteristics along. We bred for size and uniform fur quality.

We had to read up on genetics to keep abreast of new findings, but we had to remind ourselves this was a mink operation and not an experimental gene laboratory.

Breeding the generations made me think of the human race and how we have evolved. I could not help but equate mink behaviour with that of humans: some greedy, obese, vicious, some very loving, good mothers, some poor mothers, some lonely, some overactive. When I looked into the pens, I could see them all.

It seemed, as we bred the best to the best, the size of the mink decreased and the litters were much smaller. Runt mink should not be kept, because they have a small pelt and only produce more runt mink. The runts seemed to have an excess drive to reproduce while the big prize males were not as prolific.

At times, using a small syringe, we would sample semen that had been deposited in the female. We would place it on a slide, under a canvas cover with a lamp for heat, then with a microscope, examine the semen for activity.

The rancher has no way of knowing when the females

211

come into heat; only time and error establishes the cycle. But the males make a clucking sound at this time, and at the peak of breeding activity, the eager clucking makes considerable noise.

One mink shed was in view of the carport and one morning, after a few days of mating activity (taking the females to the males), I heard a roar of clucking from the males when I shut the carport door and I knew the males had by now associated the closing of the door with a day's sexual activity.

I felt like a hero entering the mink shed that day, knowing the pleasure I was about to bestow, and was greeted as such.

We sent our pelts off to market to be sold at the mercy of the auctioneer. We installed a large walk-in freezer, powered by a second Pelton wheel, a water-operated electric generation plant.

We had a large mixing tub with motor-driven paddles and a 30-inch grinder driven by a four-cylinder gas engine. Our feed came in frozen blocks the size of a cement bag – chicken waste, fish waste, off-coloured liver – and mixed cereal bags. The waste consisted of heads, legs, tails, skeletons and entrails. Our job was to feed the right percentages of each ingredient at the right time of year in a thick porridge-like mix. The mix varied according to gestation period, growth period, furring period and the winter holding diet. I found myself having to butcher many injured or unwanted horses to be ground up for mink feed – a job I did not enjoy but had learned how to do, having observed similar activity on the farm as a boy.

## A Wild Ride

Many a time a local farmer would call and offer a damaged horse for mink feed. I got a call once from Texas Riding Ranch at Mons Crossing in Whistler offering a horse. I said we'd pay $25 and the rancher said to come and pick it up.

I went in the open pick-up – no sides on the box, no plywood on the floor. We loaded the mare, a beautiful riding horse with a severe case of hoof rot, possibly because the ranch horses were out in all weather, standing in muck most of the time.

We tied the horse bridle over the cab and the engine hood to the front bumper so that the horse's neck and head extended over the cab roof. I had to drive slowly, as the horse's hooves skidded on the metal floor, particularly after it started to snow. The horse was spreading its legs to the sides of the box to keep from falling.

Finally, I came to the Lillooet Lake hydro road, then a four-wheel drive down the very steep hill. The slope was so great I could see the horse's head over the hood. I expected the horse might try to leap out of the truck and roll itself and the truck some 300 feet straight over the edge into the lake.

I went very slowly. It was a long way down the hill with the horse thrashing around, but we finally made it down.

I must confess I didn't feel good about having to shoot the horse, especially such a beautiful riding animal. I must have patted her head and said good-bye to her about three times. But I bit the bullet, as they say, and carried out the task.

## They Eat a Lot

At our peak, when we had 2,000 mink, we were feeding about 1,000 pounds of meat wastes a day plus 25 per cent cereal. To enhance this mix, we would add five per cent red meat – horse and sometimes whale meat if available. A horse would make about three weeks of supplementary feed at that rate. If horses had been our only source of meat, we would have been feeding a horse a day.

After pelting season, we kept a ratio of about one male for four females. Finally, I ended up with jet blacks, the best in the country, with the population varying from 2,000 at peak time to 400 breeders over winter. The other 1,600 went to auction.

Through the years, I had numerous pelts made into garments and hats, which brought a better price than the fur auction. I shipped my pelts to a Winnipeg furrier, who gave me the best price.

Some ranchers shipped mink liver to Seattle for use in

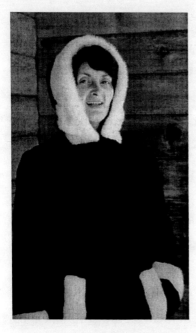

*Carol wearing a parka made from prime black Lillooet Lake mink.*

making perfume. I never did this but, even today, when I get a whiff of a woman's perfume, I can sometimes detect a trace of mink odour, partly like skunk but more pleasant.

The "furring out" of the mink is an interesting thing to see. The fall equinox signals the change of season and the winter fur sets in. As it grows, the mink sheds its summer fur.

First the winter fur sprouts on the hind feet; they look like they've got boots on. Then it climbs up the back legs, like waders, then up to the waist, looking like new pants. Finally the new fur comes up over the head, and that is when they are prime – ready for pelting. If you delay pelting, there is wear and tear and staining, which cuts the value tremendously.

## Panic in the Pens

One December 5, it snowed non-stop for two days and two nights. We had four to five feet of snow on the ground.

215

Around 7 p.m. strong winds appeared, along with heavy rain that didn't let up; I was awakened at 2 a.m. and told the main mink shed had collapsed.

We got out the lights and saw that the 200-by-40-foot shed had gone down like a pack of cards, with the aluminum roof flat on top of 400 crushed pens.

More than 200 mink escaped. About 12 were killed by the impact, but I rescued most of the others the next day, crawling on my belly in the manure. The wet manure got up my sleeves, into my gloves and soaked through my coveralls into my skin.

The mink were now in a state of considerable stress. I had spare pens around and I put them on the ground, exposing them to the weather. I put four mink in each of the pens as I caught them.

There was considerable ruckus among the crowded mink. Fights broke out among some, while others huddled together to keep warm.

Many mink hid in the woodpiles in the carport and would only show their heads. It was a curious sight to open the door, look out into the carport and see all the mink heads poking out, looking at you.

When I glanced toward the lake I thought I was seeing things. There were black streaks of mink criss-crossing over the snow crust. But I caught them and placed them in empty cereal bags. When I got close to those running around, they dove under the crust of the snow and travelled very fast like a fish under water. I could see them through the snow. To catch them, I had to pounce two feet ahead to grab them before they got farther away.

We caught all but four mink that made their way along snow ruts on the road and travelled two miles down the lake, only to be killed by a dog.

At first we thought the shed just collapsed from the weight of snow, but we found out later when cleaning up the debris, that one of the centre poles, a raw pole from the bush, had twisted grain. It snapped in half, four feet from the top, and the four-foot section pierced the ground vertically, like a spear, causing sections of the roof to collapse, each in turn, like a deck of cards.

The only thing we could do was take our breeders to a ranch in the Fraser Valley to board over the winter. We had mink transport pens, with sections just big enough for a single mink, and we stacked them in the pick-up between two-by-fours, so the mink had air and were not close enough to bite each other.

Bruce visited a pelt processing place in Surrey to hone up on skinning techniques. Believe it or not, his average time to skin a mink was two minutes, and, when timed under pressure, he could skin one in one minute.

Once the hide was peeled off, we rolled it into a ball, fur inside, and placed it in a crate like eggs in an egg box, then in the freezer, until the pelts were sent to a processing plant in Surrey for fleshing and stretching before going to auction.

They would put the pelt on a fleshing pole that resembled a tapered baseball bat, then scrape the fat off. Then they would place the pelt on a drying board and stretch it to maybe twice its size. Then it went to a ventilating room and was stored with others on a hook for auction.

I know animal rights activists protest fur ranching, claiming that the animals are treated cruelly. It is true, some ranchers used painful killing methods, and the killing bothered me, but I used the cleanest and least painful method – the neck breaker. Death is instant for the animal, and not gruesome.

Ranchers say animal farming is justified and that mink ranching does not deplete the wild stock. They liken it to fish farming, but point out it does not contaminate the wild stock. It is interesting to see activists wearing leather and eating meat while protesting.

## It Had to End

In 1972, my last year in the mink business, I once again had my mink pelts made into garments through our Winnipeg connection and got better prices than at the declining auction market.

With our three-quarters of a mile of lakefront and 128 acres of land, we were persuaded to subdivide, and we acknowledged that a mink ranch would not be compatible with a recreational retreat.

So, as they say, we pelted out, sold our equipment and pens at bargain prices, and now I missed the 4,000 eyes I was accustomed to greeting twice a day at feeding times.

At one mink convention in Winnipeg, my wife and I were seated at the dinner table with a charming French-Canadian rancher and his wife from the banks of the St. Lawrence near Quebec City.

They asked in halting English what part my wife played at the ranch. I explained she assisted with the clothespeg identification during mating seasons, one peg on the pen when the mink were paired, two pegs on the pen when they were sexually coupled, three pegs when the act was consummated (or so we hoped!).

My wife said, "I am the inspector." To which the rancher roared with laughter, saying "You are da fuck-ing inspector!" We laughed too, and had another drink.

The mink ranch days may have been over, but the drive for fur quality remains ingrained. For some years later I was driven to examine people's furs for quality. One day in a crowded elevator, the woman in front was pushed against me with her fur. I instinctively blew my breath into the fur to examine the quality. I received a startled glance back in return that said, "What kind of a creep is this?" I commented for everyone in the elevator to hear on the beautiful fur she had and explained I had been a mink rancher.

# CHAPTER 10
# RADIO WAVES

People ask who are ham radio operators and what is the lure of radio? Well, for me it all started in 1931 when I was seven and bitten by the radio bug.

We would visit family, friends and owners of early RCA or Atwater Kent radio sets. A magical tuning of an array of dials and knobs and the gathering was enthralled by Amos and Andy shows broadcast from faraway San Francisco. In Vancouver, the Daily Province newspaper operated a 10-watt transmitter, CKCD. Newscaster "Mr. Good Evening" broadcast every evening the port schedule of the "good ship Maquinna" of the Canadian Pacific Steamships, alerting Vancouver Island's west coast residents to the expected delivery of mail and supplies. To me another far away place reached by mysterious radio waves.

In Bonnyville, Alberta, at age 10, I was thrilled to hear a radio receiving an Edmonton station. In Mission, B.C., it

*Home base station antenna.*

was the radios tuned to CHWK in Chilliwack. I was thoroughly hooked and the fascination kept growing.

In 1939, radio ham VE5KX, Herb Colcough, showed me the transmitter that he built by fastening radio parts to a table top. I couldn't wait until I could do the same and communicate all over the world by voice or Morse Code.

School and I parted company at age 15, and I went to work in the radio repair business. From then on, it was radio and more radio. At 16 I attended Sprott Shaw Radio School in Vancouver and at 17 trained in the air force as a wireless operator and radio repair technician. My Morse Code speed climbed to 30 words a minute (15 was a pass and special certificates were issued to those who qualified with speeds of 25 words per minute).

In 1945, at end of the war, I was granted my Radio Amateur Certificate of Proficiency. Not much in life excited me more than the prospect of constructing my own station and getting on the air. Soon I was installing and repairing radiotelephones on small ships and up coastal camps but even the job of my dreams didn't equal the satisfaction of

222

*A meeting of the Point Grey Amateur Radio Club at Lillooet Lake in May 1995.*
*My membership dates from 1948 when I lived on Belmont Avenue in Vancouver.*

operating my first ham station.

My present call sign is VE7 CHN, the VE standing for Canada and the 7 for British Columbia. CHN is my individual identifier.

## We're Connected

My home station is in a small room in our Lillooet Lake home, the "ham shack" as the fraternity calls home stations, but I also have equipment in our houseboat on the lake and in the car.

From the first at Lillooet Lake, Jean, my first wife, and I used ham radio to keep contact from Vancouver to the lake. Jean, who had been a wireless operator in the air force had also become a registered ham operator in 1946. As her second call she had been issued the coveted call sign VE7 YL

223

by friend and radio inspector Jim Kitchen. YL stood for Young Lady, the term used for women operators, probably not politically correct today but still in use on the air.

*The radio amateur fraternity is international. Here is Kenji Sujimoto broadcasting from his ham station in Tokyo. Japanese signals often flood B.C. air waves.*

YLs were not that plentiful, and when Jean called CQ, CQ, CQ on the popular 10-metre band, American hams would line up to talk to her. Many were ex-GIs, and since she had been in the service here, they had a lot in common to talk about. She completed many a phone patch for the American forces in Japan. During the disastrous 1948 Fraser River flood, Jean was out on the dikes in our vehicle with a hand-built mobile unit directing emergency radio traffic.

## *May Day!*

The ham fraternity has a long-standing commitment to provide radio communications in every kind of emergency. Just a couple of summers ago the call "Medical Emergency – May Day – May Day" intruded on our lazy afternoon chat on the 75-metre band Retired Gentlemen's net.

It was a call not many of us had heard before but by tradition and training were ready to handle. My old friend Les Saul, VE7 GBT, retired TV newsman, former navy signalman, long-time ham operator and emergency net controller, picked up the call at his home station on Thetis Island, and closed down the net to work on the emergency. "Stand by," he called. "Stand by to relay signals if required." The rest of us waited and listened as the drama unfolded. It all went better than might have been expected.

The call sign was KB7 DZV, a United States call issued to Mark Downing of Portland, Oregon. Mark, working with a mobile transmitter from Chief Matthews Bay south of Kemano, gave a May Day call on our net frequency because he could hear us faintly and hoped we might hear him. I knew the area well, a tough place for radio signals, as I had found out in the early 1950s providing communication equipment for the Kemano power project of the Aluminum Company of Canada.

*VE7CHN, Houseboat Marine, fitted with antennae for all amateur bands.*

Mark said later he broke into the chatter and after several calls he could hear Les tell the rest of us to stand by because he thought he could hear the May Day coming in.

They finally made

contact, with us all monitoring, and Mark was able to give the global positioning location: 53.20.221 North Latitude; 128.07.623 West Longitude. He reported that a young woman had fallen from the second storey of a lodge building she was helping put up for an environmental group. The woman, Jamie Saunt, 20, a volunteer worker from Pennsylvania, was lying injured and in pain, and her companions had no way of moving her or helping her.

*Les Saul, VE7 GBT, Thetis Island veteran radio amateur operator. Les operated the coastal boaters' net for many years and has handled numerous emergencies. Boaters check in daily by radio to report on location, weather, any problems and to exchange messages.*

Mark reported she had a back injury and possible concussion, and asked for help. Before long, Les had arranged for the Rescue Coordinator Centre to dispatch a helicopter and paramedics and airlift the woman to a hospital in Terrace. She had broken her pelvis, we were told afterwards.

Mark, a craftsman and woodworker volunteer with Ecotrust, which was building the lodge as a joint project with the Haisla First Nation, had kind words for us later. He recalled that the signals became stronger as antennae were pointed in his direction, and he was impressed with the rescue operation.

"I still get goose bumps when I remember how the helicopter hovered at the river mouth with its runners just touching the bank," Mark recalled. "It couldn't land because the tide had come up, and its rotors were spinning right beside the lodge building.

"So it hung there while the paramedics jumped out, examined Jamie and bundled her in."

## It Started with Tinkering

This is just an example of how amateur radio interfaces with society in time of need. Floods, earthquakes, tornadoes, hurricanes destroy established communication links. At the flip of a switch, amateur stations are ready to operate, filling the gap until public and commercial facilities are re-established, then completing the job by locating missing persons and contacting family members.

A public service net is active in each Canadian province. In 1998, during the big ice storm in Quebec and Ontario, hams were at the ready providing emergency communication.

Our Canadian peacekeepers have ham stations. Astronauts never leave home without theirs. Ham clubs have provided thousands of schoolchildren the opportunity to talk to satellites and the Mir space station as they whiz by overhead.

For 55 years I have been a radio amateur, one of many

who became fascinated by radio waves that could be transmitted and captured over great distances. Advancement of the art was driven by those bitten by the radio bug; experimenters, technicians, pilots, engineers and those who could see profit in the future.

My lifetime enthusiasm has given me satisfying careers in many aspects of radio and introduced me to interesting people the world over.

*Radio amateur operators frequently exchange QSL cards confirming long distance (DX) contacts made on the air. Most ham stations feature a display of these colourful reminders of conversations held with hams all over the world from the North Pole to the South Pole.*

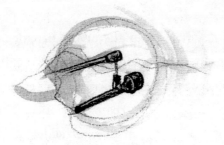

# CHAPTER 11
# MOUNTAIN FM – THE BEGINNING

What were we doing applying for a Radio Broadcast licence? What did we know about a radio station? Well, I had the technical knowledge and Carol and I had the will to make it work. We felt confident that we could learn whatever else we needed to know.

What we did know at the time, the late '70s, was that there was no road or weather information for travellers between Pemberton, let alone Lillooet Lake, and Vancouver. Vancouver was 150 km away, and the broadcast signals that came and went with changing condi-

*Some of the Mountain FM shareholders meeting to discuss licence applications to the CRTC. Left to right: Connie Cleaver, Fred Wiley, Ralph Dunbar, Carol Potvin, Al Cleaver and Louis Potvin.*

*Tony Gardiner, P eng, prepared CRTC engineering briefs for all seven Mountain FM radio transmitter stations.*

tions never mentioned Pemberton or Squamish. Whistler was referred to only rarely, as a "pie in the sky project."

Vancouver broadcasters hadn't really considered the future Sea to Sky corridor as territory inhabited by regular people. That began to change when slides blocked the road and bridges began washing out on the Squamish Highway and it became labelled "the Killer Highway." We needed local current road and weather information.

Carol and I knew this only too well. All our building, mechanical and personal supplies had to be brought from Vancouver. When we left Lillooet Lake on weekly – often

*The Moloughney Building, home of the Mountain FM broadcast studios in Squamish.*

twice-weekly – runs for cement, machinery parts, explosives, building materials for the mill and subdivision, we had no idea what conditions we would encounter along the way.

At the CRTC office in Vancouver, I put forth my plan to establish radio broadcast facilities for Squamish, Whistler and Pemberton. Squamish, the only commercial retail centre, would have the community studio and main transmitter, with rebroads (relay stations that rebroadcast signals to extend coverage) in Whistler and Pemberton.

Virginia Krapiec listened attentively, sizing me up, and said, "Would you like to review a recent successful application approved for CISL-AM Richmond?" After reviewing these documents, I was informed I could write to the CRTC in Hull, Quebec and request application forms. Later when these arrived, we were taken aback by the requirements. Market surveys, station format, promise of performance, financial capability, personal history, letters of support, and engineering briefs were some of the application data the CRTC required before a public hearing could be called.

*Mike Dickinson, successful applicant for CISL Richmond, offering encouragement to Carol Potvin during CRTC hearing.*

231

We immediately began a survey of businesses in Squamish, Whistler, and Pemberton, and canvassed residents by phone and in person about their views on a local radio station. The feedback was positive with many people offering their help. Dr. Laverne Kindree, an alderman, introduced me to the Squamish Rotary Club. While the reception was positive, some said radio wouldn't work in this area; too many power lines. Others said, "We heard it all before, we will believe it when we see it." But the Squamish Council voted wholeheartedly to support our CRTC application.

Once we had started beating the bushes in Whistler, letting it be known we had a CRTC application underway, another group emerged claiming they too were proposing a radio station. This application was for Whistler only, excluding Squamish and Pemberton. The Whistler Council and some groups supported the idea of a Whistler-only radio station because it was home-grown, but most went on record supporting any application for this much-needed service. In fact, we received only a lukewarm reception at Whistler.

Pemberton, our home turf, extended considerable support, although some council members expressed little interest in our proposal. Mayor Shirley Henry of Pemberton had the foresight to see the potential benefits of a corridor radio station serving three communities. So much so, Mayor

Henry and her husband George were among our early investors. Bob and Pat Priest of the Pemberton Pharmacy thought the idea was wonderful and they too threw in their support and became investors. It is interesting to note these Pemberton folks were among the few who were interested in the development of the area and who expressed their confidence in Carol and myself as being capable of bringing it about.

We were without success in obtaining investors from the Whistler area, finding most people we talked to there were looking for a quick return, and the

*Jonathan Brett, operations manager, about to climb Hospital Hill to the Squamish transmitter site.*

concept of serving the corridor was of no interest to them. Even in Squamish, where there was lots of public interest, we could not get those who professed to be civic-minded to invest ever so little into our radio station project. We found this disheartening, as many we called upon were involved in numerous other high-profile community activities.

We were not short on popular potential listener support. Out of the blue, Mayor Jim Elliott of Squamish drove out to the Lillooet Lake office one weekend, said, "I hear you are looking for investors for a radio station," and then and there dropped a cheque on my desk and left. We sought further investors from the lot owners at our Heather Jean

*In the studio reception area listening to the first sweet sounds of Mountain FM Radio.*
*Left to right: Christy Vidler, Ian Alexander, Louis Potvin, Suzanne St. Pierre, Chuck*
*McCoy, Jeff Vidler.*

Properties on Lillooet Lake and welcomed Tom and Elsie Linning, as well as Al and Connie Cleaver and Fred and Eileen Wiley as further investors. The more community investors, the less Mountain FM would have to borrow from the bank. Cloudesley Hoodspith, publisher of the Squamish Times, had tried to get a radio application off the ground for Squamish and insisted he too become an investor.

At that time, the CRTC did not look kindly at newspapers being involved in radio station ownership, but as the Hoodspith investment would be minor, it did not pose a problem for our application.

Members of Carol's family were big financial supporters. Our daughter Michelle with husband Roger, son Paul, and Carol's dad and mom, Bob and Maisie invested in our dream – by this time our obsession. Starting from scratch would be costly. Paul also lent his valuable professional help preparing market research data for CRTC applications.

234

Having a radio technical background was a tremendous advantage to me; it enabled me to understand what could be done with FM radio. I knew that FM, which broadcasts on very high frequencies, would cut out the static that plagues the AM band, and I was sure that, although VHF signals travel on a "line of sight," they would also go around corners by bouncing off the mountains. We finally firmed up our proposal for a major FM transmitter in Squamish, one mountainside station in Whistler and another in Pemberton. Engineering briefs for each station were needed to illustrate coverage. A description of the "footprint" had to be submitted to the Ministry of Communication engineers for frequency assignment and power limitation. Stations within the 100-mile zone on either side of the Canada-U.S. border require special frequency coordination between the two countries. You get channel A, we get channel B, etc.

In December 1980, the CRTC called a hearing at the Hyatt Regency Hotel in Vancouver to hear our application for Squamish, Whistler, and Pemberton and that of the other applicant for a low power FM station for Whistler only. The days before the hearing were hectic, as we memorized as much data as possible. The hearing went well; our presentation well received, with the commissioner asking pertinent questions about our Federal Business Development Bank Financing, and whether we would put more money into the endeavour should the need arise.

Positive interveners spoke of the need for such a broadcast facility. Alderman Kindree; Dan Cumming, chairperson of the Squamish Lillooet Regional District; and Mayor Shirley Henry of Pemberton all made presentations. Mayor Pat Carlton of Whistler spoke at the hearing on behalf of the Whistler applicant, but their prospects did not look promising. The mayor made it clear the council supported the local applicant, but they wished it known they supported any successful applicant. The hearing continued on into the night.

*Bob Storey, broadcast consultant, helped us prepare for questioning by the CRTC Commissioners at the public hearing for the Squamish Whistler Pemberton broadcast license.*

At a late hour, Terrill Patterson of Squamish arrived to intervene. Patterson was a local critic of municipal politics and most other things in Squamish. The chair queried why he didn't intervene in the normal process as advertised in the Squamish paper. Patterson's answer was that he felt the local paper's reporting was too one-sided, and he wanted to know if he would get equal air time to reply to anything the future radio station would report which he felt incorrect.

"Certainly, we would give equal air time and if Mr. Patterson chose air time at this same late hour, we would give him double time," I replied. (This was easy because air time at night is far from prime listening time.)

Upon that note, the hearing was adjourned. Our supporters met for a late dinner in Vancouver, everyone keyed up in anticipation of a favourable future decision from the CRTC.

A new player slipped into the place at the table beside our daughter Suzanne. Suzanne had done the sales survey work for our application and would be sales representative for the new station. The newcomer was Chuck McCoy, brother to our newly chosen station manager Jeff Vidler. Chuck was destined to take Suzanne away to Winnipeg where he was programming head of Moffat Broadcasting's Canada-wide stations. In return we received immeasurable professional help and advice and three wonderful grandchildren.

## We Had to Work Fast

We were not too long in waiting. The CRTC phoned in the spring of 1981, to tell us our application had been approved. We had to move and fast. Our promise of performance stated we would be on air within 12 months. The first effort was to establish our Squamish station.

Hospital Hill had been selected as the transmitter site. George Miller, land surveyor was put to work locating turn-of-the-century survey markers. Our site was on large rocks overlooking Squamish, an excellent location for propagation of radio signals. An abandoned logging railway was all

237

*Shelley Wright, the voice of the morning show on Mountain FM's first broadcast day, November 30, 1981*

grown over and there was no easy access to the upper half of the hill. It was a tough climb. The tower crew was taken in by helicopter. The transmitter building was so heavy we had to bring in a larger helicopter from Abbotsford airport.

We had to string a hydro pole line to the site. The rocky surface called for drilling at each pole site. Hydro poles were fitted on the ground with brackets, insulator at the top and a large steel pin at the base of each pole, allowing the helicopter to drop each pole in place individually. The high-voltage cables were strung on the poles and dropped to the transmitter building.

Before all this could be done, the right-of-way had to be cleared. Two capable chain-saw operators from Mount Currie, Ralph Dan and Harry Dick, who worked for us at Lillooet Lake, took care of the tricky job. Joe LaVenture's Chieftain Hotel put them up, offering two pieces of blueberry pie for dessert each night, and we were soon ready for the installation crew.

Studio premises were found in a new, not-yet-completed commercial building close to the small retail market area of Squamish. Bob and Jane Moloughney, the building owners, had built living quarters on the third floor which were occupied by Jane's mother and her cat. Later the apartment was occupied by successive on-air types.

Sometimes we feared for our licence. CRTC regulations were all-encompassing and rigid; it was difficult for small stations to comply. Many of the requirements were costly. On-air talent was needed because very little prerecorded material was allowed. What was allowed was too expensive to purchase or to produce.

In the Moloughney building we set up a newsroom, on-air studio, production studio, workshop area, sales offices and reception area. S.W. Davis Broadcast Consultants supplied an excellent technical crew to design and install the on-air facilities. Mike Fawcett and George Sumi worked against the clock. We had a CRTC deadline to meet.

To oversee the set-up and manage the on-air function of the station, we had hired the talented young broadcaster, Jeff Vidler. This was Jeff's first opportunity in station management and he wasn't about to blow it. Jeff gave it all he had and more. Opening day rolled around, all on-air people ready and advertising bookings in place. The day before opening, Jeff was drained of energy, butterflies in his stomach, and in no shape for opening day. I packed him off to the Bayshore Hotel in Vancouver for a peaceful break before the culmination of all our efforts.

### "We Have a Radio Station"

Everything was organized, so it was easy for Carol and

me to take charge. At 5:00 a.m., outside the back door, we greeted our morning show person, Shelley Wright, who had butterflies in her stomach as well. A friendly hug reassured us both that we would do just fine. No butterflies for our cool, experienced newsman, Jim Johnson, who had worked with other stations including the CBC.

Six a.m. came around, you could feel all the FM radios in Squamish tuned to our frequency of 104.9 FM Mhz. At exactly 6:00 a.m., we went on air. "Good morning, this is Jim Johnson with the news from Mountain FM studios in Squamish."

"Wow," I said looking at Carol, "we have a radio station."

Shelley Wright had a wonderful first day on air. The telephone rang constantly with congratulations. Carol and I felt good and our staff began to relax and enjoy our "open house visitors."

We had sent out invitations for an opening night reception to be held in the hallway of the unfinished building, with small groups touring the studio facilities. Jonathan Brett, our program director, fastened several microphone cords together to reach the guests in the hallway and I did interviews every ten minutes or so. When I broadcast, "This is Louis Potvin coming to you from the studios of Mountain FM in downtown Squamish," logging operator Norm Barr and his wife chuckled at the downtown Squamish description, saying "maybe someday."

That was November 1981 and look at Squamish today.

*Mayor Jim Elliott cuts the ribbon officially marking the opening of Mountain FM Radio coverage of Squamish and the Sea to Sky Highway. Left to right: Mayor Elliott, Carol and Louis Potvin, Jeff Vidler. Photo credit: Colin Baxter*

We enjoyed a great turnout in miserable rain and wet snow. Whistler people declined our invitations but the head of the Chamber of Commerce, Michael D'Artois, called extending his congratulations, explaining Whistler people felt the radio headquarters should have been in Whistler and this was a Squamish affair. But Squamish had been chosen as the economic base. Whistler at that time was still a dream. Also, people didn't understand that the propagation of our signal had to commence from Squamish, if we were ever to have a station in Whistler.

Pemberton supporters Shirley and George Henry and Bob and Pat Priest caught in a snowstorm in the Cheakamus Canyon kept in touch with the proceedings by car radio, arriving in time to enjoy the evening's affairs. Jeff, our recovered station manager, returned early evening full of energy and grabbed the mike from me, saying, "I can handle things now." The ceremonies ended with dinner at the Chieftain Hotel. From here on, it was 24-hour-a-day broadcasting.

The Squamish market was small, really not large enough to support its own radio station but we were counting on the growth potential of the Squamish-Whistler-Pemberton corridor. Immediately after we went on air, the B.C. recession of the early '80s hit and hit hard. What a time to open a radio station!

## *Lessons for us All*

Contrary to what many of our listeners believed, advertising is the lifeblood of broadcasting. Some thought we were funded by the government, and as taxpayers, they should call the tune. But alas, we were not the CBC and had to pay our way.

The Mountain FM sales staff used their ingenuity to prepare advertising packages the merchants could afford. The on-air crew promoted community affairs: Squamish Days, logger sports, Chamber activities, school info, council meetings, fundraisers, sporting events, garage sales. Residents had access to air time.

Whistler and Pemberton had local residents on air every morning with their own weather reports and events.

Whatever happened, we tried to be there, perhaps not as professional as we and our listeners would have liked, but striving and full of enthusiasm. Remote broadcast equipment was designed and assembled in our own workshop to go into a neat silver-painted lunch bucket.

*Mike Killeen and Johnathan Brett, on-air personalities in the early days.*

The production staff prepared documentation of Squamish and the corridor and its future potential. The Chamber of Commerce ran a contest to name the highway, the only road link to the outside world. The Duffy Lake road north and east to the Fraser Canyon was still a gravel endurance test. On-air we promoted the "Sea to Sky Highway" until the young, old and indifferent knew the name better than their own.

During the winter, road reports throughout the day and night were a necessity as bridge washouts, rock slides and closures were common on the Sea to Sky Highway. In the early '80s, we got up-to-date weather and road information from logging truck, tow truck and bus drivers and put them on the air. This was before the cell phone era but we soon had installed our own VHF radio system. Road conditions affected everyone. Listeners called in for road reports before setting out in bad weather.

At first, Mountain FM news reports were pretty unsettling to many locals, even council members. To be quoted or

*Stephanie Hudson, our 'no-nonsense' news reporter covered local affairs.*

to hear your actions reported by our tough, tell-it-as-it-is news director, Stephanie Hudson, was a far cry from a story in the weekly paper written by friendly acquaintances. Listeners enjoyed the news as long as it was not about themselves. For a while Stephanie kept me busy meeting agitated listeners.

One morning I interviewed a controversial new alderman. On my way to lunch, a husky-looking merchant came up and threatened, "If you ever put that guy on air again I'm going to plough you one." A local biker was involved in an incident and charged by the police, which we reported. That evening a biker tossed a rock through the studio window and fled. Others mentioned on-air complained to the CRTC.

Handling the news in a small community is a responsibility. It takes a certain courage to report fairly and honestly and with compassion. I was a novice in the broadcast world but learning fast.

# CHAPTER 12
# THE WILD WORLD OF
# BROADCASTING

Mountain FM slowly settled into a routine, broadcasting to the Squamish coverage area from our studio in the Moloughney Building. I relaxed a bit and looked to the next set of requirements.

The terms of our broadcast licences called for Mountain FM coverage of Whistler within six months and Pemberton in 12 months. That meant on-air pick-up of the Squamish transmitter signal by a Whistler receiver in turn to be rebroadcast to the Whistler area and to a Pemberton trans-mitter. There the signal would be rebroadcast to the Pemberton-Mount Currie area. We needed two receiver/transmitter sites with towers for antennae and buildings for equipment located high enough to pick up a strong incoming Mountain FM signal.

Well, Carol had told the CRTC hearing that in our part

*The Whistler transmitter building under construction. Clive Camm up the tower adjusting the antenna.*

of the world, if you want something done, you do it yourself. And that's what we did.

On Whistler Mountain, adjacent to B.C. Rail's microwave site, we found our Whistler transmitter home. It was a tough access by road in summer, and by snowmobile and helicopter in winter but the site provided the crucial highway coverage. Whistler at this time had about 1,200 residents, not much of a market. Advertisers targeted their message to skiers and local residents as they travelled the highway; the news department delivered the vital road and snow reports.

Engineering briefs outline projected signal paths, so it looked simple in the office. But in the field it was a tricky business locating a receiver for on-air pick-up of the transmitted signal. Radio waves are notoriously fickle, not always covering an area solidly, often missing small pockets and corners of the terrain.

In preparing our Whistler installation, gaining access in

the deep winter snow was the first priority. I knew from experience that power outages and equipment failures weren't likely to occur exclusively on sunny summer days, so I designed a two-room building, the outer room a winter entrance with a split door. We could tunnel through the snow to reach the top half of the door, slide down in the outer room and enter the warm, dry transmitter-equipment room.

Construction materials were left-over lumber and roofing material from our Lillooet Lake cabin-building projects. The building took

*Digging down to the Whistler split-door entrance way, an exercise performed many times that first winter as we learned how our equipment reacted in the cold and wind of the mountain top.*

shape all neat and cozy, ready for the heavy snowfalls above Whistler Village and the all-important highway.

Erecting and rigging the tower became a technical training exercise for our on-air staff. Working for Mountain FM held some surprises; whether it was in your life plan or not, you learned the basics of radio transmission as well as the more glamorous on-air skills. Clive Camm, Barry Forward, Jonathan Brett, Owen Searle and more, all worked their hearts out on our transmitter and tower installations in

*Enjoying the Pemberton celebration, our daughter and shareholder Michelle Marino and Mount Currie Chief Baptiste Ritchie.*

Whistler, and later Bowen Island, and three more transmitters on the Sunshine Coast.

Many of the staff were young people who were brand new graduates of the BCIT radio broadcasting program. Radio seems to attract those with endless enthusiasm and passion. Not many considered it just a job. The passion wasn't confined to career paths, it spilled over into life, love and adventure. All those creative minds brewed some pretty high octane at times. Some days we thought the TV series "WKRP" wasn't too far off the mark.

Radio business is show business. Projecting your personality is a big part of what you do and the search to do that is endless. Every incoming mail brought us demo tapes from people who wanted to work for us, and our people were sending out demos looking for a larger audience.

Big contributions were made to the station by these passionate people. I only wish I could remember them all by name. But their energy I'll not forget.

## Hunting for Signals

Once the Whistler signal was on air, it was Pemberton's turn. Locating a suitable receiving and broadcasting site

248

meant Carol and I hiked around through the bushes and trees in likely spots carrying a portable antenna and radio. Once a possible site was found, it was back to the car for a ladder to act as a test tower. It was a good thing that we enjoyed outdoor life, for there was lots of it waiting for us.

We found the perfect spot, obtained the necessary permits and commenced work with the help of Pemberton friends George and Michael Henry preparing the concrete foundation and Wayne Ferguson erecting the tower and antenna. Meanwhile, I converted the box of an old truck we had used for worker transportation during the mill years. Before long it was transformed into a handsome transmitter building. For very little money, we were ready to hit the Pemberton air waves.

Mountain FM's opening night at the Legion in Pemberton saw Mayor Shirley Henry cut the ribbon in a crowd of supporters including Bob and Pat Priest. Pat was all primed to give us her daily on-air reports of Pemberton

*Pemberton CISP opening, left to right, Pat and Bob Priest, Jonathan Brett, Mayor Shirley Henry cutting the ribbon, Carol and Louis Potvin, October 1982.*

news and weather, starting the very next morning. Present and future Mount Currie Chiefs Ritchie, Leonard Andrew and Fraser Andrew were there. Everyone was happy, Pemberton residents were gaining a voice in the Sea to Sky corridor and we had fulfilled our promise to the CRTC. Many congratulatory letters arrived at the station and the CRTC offices. I felt we were making a real connection with our listeners.

We had achieved a major engineering success and proven the skeptics wrong. Mountain FM was now heard the length of the Sea to Sky Highway from Horseshoe Bay in West Vancouver to Pemberton. Our dream of one unifying voice for the communities of the corridor had come true. Next on the agenda was making it an economic success.

## Hunting for Revenue

For now, in the midst of British Columbia's tough recession of the '80s, we had to meet the challenge to survive economically. It was the failure of B.C.'s number-one moneymaker, the forest industry, that had sparked the recession. Nearly all B.C. business was dependent on the well-being of the forestry giants. And none more so than the Sea to Sky corridor, boasting only logging-related endeavours and the first stirrings of the recreational boom of the future.

Whistler was struggling to get going. After a time, the provincial government saved the day by creating and fund-

*Jim Johnston, newsman, first voice on Mountain FM, 6:00 am, Nov 30, 1981.*

ing the Resort Municipality of Whistler. But for now, Whistler merchants were walking away from their outstanding accounts.

Visionary Whistler entrepreneurs were caught in an almost impossible situation trying to establish businesses for the future. Many didn't make it and were taken over by a second wave of believers.

Squamish workers were moving to greener fields, the radio market was shrinking and programming demands were increasing. Our listeners wanted a big city sound, and so did we, but what to do?

Fortunately, the barter system came to life, deals were made, meals and station vehicles were exchanged for radio advertising time.

The CRTC was our master, threatening licence cancellation for creative solutions. Our Promise of Performance tied us into unalterable formats and services. In spite of strong listener controversy, we broadcast religious programming, pleasing some listeners and displeasing others, but the shows paid the rent. Besides, the sponsors didn't walk away from their commitments.

A larger revenue base was essential; our market was just too small. Across Howe Sound was the Sunshine Coast, an area not unlike our own; semi-isolated, three small popula-

251

tion centres and no local radio voice. Best of all, I was sure a Squamish signal could be rebroadcast from Bowen Island at the entrance to Howe Sound, which meant we could beam Mountain FM programming to the Sunshine Coast.

## On to the Sunshine Coast

Once again Carol and I took to the woods to search for a receiver site on Bowen Island. We were struggling through wet salal underbrush holding aloft a six-foot wide antenna and carrying a portable radio when a deer hunter with bow drawn appeared silently through the trees. We had been stalked as prey, but Carol spotted him and we identified ourselves in time. They say there are dangers inherent in every business.

Just beyond the hunter was a large boulder in a small clearing and there we found what we were searching for, a steady Mountain FM signal.

Studying the Sunshine Coast as a future broadcasting area, it was apparent why there was no local radio station. The terrain wouldn't allow a single transmitter to cover the area. American, Vancouver, and

*Barry Forward, our intrepid newsman, on firm ground at the base of the Bowen Island transmitting tower.*

252

Vancouver Island signals sailed in unobstructed over the water. Lots of radio signals but no local news or programming.

To test what we could do with FM in this area, I quickly constructed an FM antenna and placed it on my desk. I pruned it to the exact length to resonate to the operating frequency, and to my dismay the heat generated by the radio frequency melted a neat imprint on my padded desktop, radio frequency being a close cousin to the microwave. At least I knew it would work, because the antenna was hot.

My brother-in-law Bob Roycroft and his wife (another Carol), who was our office accountant, volunteered to help. This was their kind of fun. In the cold November rain and wet snow, they dragged their small travel trailer to the top of Antenna Hill on Bowen Island to rebroadcast a test signal.

No licence, no experimenting is the rule. This was definitely a CRTC "no-no" performed in the middle of the night. Carol and I drove furtively along the Sunshine Coast Highway in a snowstorm recording signal strengths transmitted from the dark of Bowen Island by Bob and Carol in their lonely little trailer.

The CRTC heard our application and in the summer of 1984, granted Mountain FM licences for rebroadcast stations at Bowen Island, Sechelt, Pender Harbour and later Egmont.

The multi-talented Mountain FM crew was conscripted again to dig, hammer, paint, mix concrete, climb towers and

*Pender Harbour transmitter tower and antennae being air-lifted to Cecil Mountain site.*

install antennae for each of the four rebroad sites.

Barry Forward was chosen to head the Sunshine Coast news and programming studio. I thought it only fitting he should be the one to assist with the Bowen Island installation. After all, that's where the Sunshine Coast signal would originate; it's always helpful to know the business from the ground up.

Barry was pretty nervous of heights, and the tower was 60 feet high, facing the rocky seashore below. Also, Barry had mixed the concrete for the tower footings, his first-ever cement job. And he was not sure the mix was strong enough. And his job of climbing the tower and affixing the antennae presented a number of problems: how to hold on, use tools and balance long, heavy pieces of equipment all at the same time.

I could see no difficulty in this, and once Barry was in place, shouted orders for different alignments and placements. This was in Barry's "before glasses" days. He maintains he wouldn't have been able to identify the Sunshine

Coast even if he dared take his gaze off the tower.

But the intrepid newsman triumphed, the signal flew in the right direction, the tower remained standing.

The Pender Harbour site on Cecil Mountain was the toughest. Cold, wet, marginal flying days plagued the installation work. On such an October day, Sechelt Helicopters lowered supplies and the transmitter building (home-made of course) to the site. When the concrete pad was ready, the tower was lowered to our willing crew, Wayne Ferguson (Pemberton friend and electronic whiz), Barry Forward, Carol, and Miguel Guevara, our caretaker from the lake.

## Miguel Looked for a Signal Too

Miguel had escaped from El Salvador after the death squad had come calling to his home. He made his way to the U.S. When the Americans threatened to deport him, he was sponsored by the United Church and found himself in Pemberton. Church members heard I could communicate in basic Spanish and asked if we could give him a job, and he became our caretaker.

The church tried to alleviate his lonely existence at the lake and invited him to their regular poetry reading group, which was in English, although he spoke only Spanish. Miguel liked the ladies a lot and the group was mostly ladies. Every week Miguel looked in vain for a "signal" from any one of them but reported all the "signals" were for Reverend

York, amateur poet and established ladies' man.

Through necessity, I had added lobbyist and mountain climber to my list of "jack-of-all-trades." It had taken some manoeuvering to obtain the necessary allocations for the new sites. It seemed if I wasn't donning my one suit and tie for a meeting or hearing with some government department, I was climbing or helicoptering to the top of a mountain.

### *Musical Programming*

Implementing our Sunshine Coast service was complicated by the mystery of the musical notes. We had an innovative dial tone switch that allowed the Sechelt studio to cut out the main Mountain FM programming from Squamish to permit local Sunshine Coast broadcasting.

But the trouble was the tones were being triggered by on-air musical selections. We made many trips back and

*The Sunshine Coast trailer office/studio at Wilson Creek, moved later to Sechelt. Frequency sign 104.7 is backed by 107.1 for travelers coming from opposite direction.*

256

forth to the Bowen transmitter trying different tones, more tones, different combinations. But each time we would go off the air when a recording would duplicate the tones. Using tones for switching was pretty advanced at that time, so we had to go far afield for help. On the advice of an Ontario engineer, I settled on four tones with gates of shorter intervals (the time between tones).

*Mountain FM ski team displaying sponsors' skis, David Larsen, Wayne Broomfield, Clive Camm.*

This solved the problem. At last our music programming didn't bring the whole Sunshine Coast network crashing down. Some listeners said our choice of music was capable of causing far worse things. Satisfying musical tastes of listeners is a recognized impossibility in radio, although an inordinate amount of time and money is spent trying to please.

Seven transmitter sites perched on mountainsides miles and ferry rides apart presented quite a challenge for maintenance and repairs. Emergency outages went hand-in-hand with nasty weather and even if the helicopters could fly, it was too costly to use them, except as a last resort.

I frequently found myself crawling through the wet snow on hands and knees the last few hundred slippery yards to

257

the Squamish site. On one such trip I discovered the answer to a long-standing problem of going off air on blustery, wet days. Experts had failed to diagnose the problem although we spent thousands of dollars on consulting fees.

As I sat resting from my climb, a gust of wind rattled the radome antenna enclosure, releasing a waterfall from overhead. I scrambled up the tower and poked my screwdriver through the drain hole screen. Out came mushy lumps of a hornet nest, which had plugged the hole and allowed a buildup of rainwater to short the elements and knock us off the air.

On another one of those wet, stormy nights, Carol learned the versatility of the midnight to 6:00 a.m. programming feed we purchased from Selkirk Broadcasting and plugged in every night as did most small stations throughout B.C. With daughter Michelle and granddaughter Gillian, Carol was on the road to Squamish when she had car trouble. In those days, by 6 p.m. Squamish was a dead city, no stores open, no services, no life on the streets. Using the Mountain FM VHF system from car to studio, Carol called the evening on-air person, Don Molson, to get help. "Oh, no problem, I'll come to you myself," he said.

To keep the station broadcasting in his absence, he hooked up the live CKWX programming. So that evening, our listeners were treated to Big-City Sound over Mountain FM air waves.

# The Big Balloon Caper

Promotion is a huge part of radio broadcasting. The station and advertisers are promoted with every game and gimmick the promotions department can invent. Independent businesses also package and sell promotions to stations but I liked to try something we could do ourselves.

A neighbour at Lillooet Lake, Teruo Kubota, was a balloonist, a record-holder at that. So I knew his advice would be good. "A big helium balloon to float above the grand Squamish celebration, Loggers' Sports Day." Right away I could see it floating up there displaying Mountain FM in giant letters. Teruo supplied the balloon, forgetting to fill us in on a few things, such as the necessity of a strong-enough anchor to hold it against the infamous Squamish wind.

We didn't have any idea what we were getting into. We tethered the balloon to a large pole that had been put up for the event, but it started blowing around as soon as it began to rise. So we tied it to Mountain FM reporter Clive Camm's Subaru station wagon, the chain link fence and everything else in sight. But we couldn't hold it, even though several of us were scrambling around desperately, pulling on different ropes each time the wind changed direction.

Two burly bystanders tried to cut the anchor ropes with their knives but I couldn't have that because the balloon would have soared away.

So I called the starter to shoot the balloon down with his

*Clive Camm and Louis Potvin feeling pretty confident just before launching the big promotional helium balloon.*

gun. It just slowly softened and sagged into the top branches of a tall tree.

One of the loggers there to compete in the sports climbed up and brought it down.

The Sunshine Coast listenership grew slowly against the competition of the professional Vancouver programming that saturated the airwaves. Squamish on-air personality Clive Camm moved to Sechelt and was developing a strong local morning show from our "do-it-ourselves" studio trailer. One of our frequent callers was Gordon Wilson, later to become MLA for the area and a prominent figure in B.C. politics.

Sales were picking up. In the Sea to Sky corridor too, confidence was growing with our creeping progress. We were feeling good and settled down to enjoy the broadcast business.

# CHAPTER 13
# RAISING OUR VOICE

Try as we all did, we were caught in the classic small business dilemma, grow or fade away. Everyone pitched in but we couldn't compensate for what we had, a small market waiting for a big boom.

Looking at our coverage area for inspiration we could see the Sea to Sky corridor and the Sunshine Coast were, in reality, both 100-mile cul de sacs starting and ending on Vancouver's North Shore. North and West Vancouver were the big city shopping spots for our listeners, a truth we rarely alluded to on the air.

Upset local merchants had converged on the station after one young woman had confided chattily on air that she was going to West Vancouver to do her Christmas shopping.

I did my own shopping, searching for a "sovereignty association" with a Vancouver station or cable network but

the city folk just wanted to gobble us up and I wasn't ready for that yet.

I was sure we should apply for a licence to broadcast to North and West Vancouver. With the extended coverage we could take our listeners from one end of the two established traffic patterns to the other.

In an unprecedented coup, we got approval from the B.C. Minister of Highways, Alex Fraser, to install our FM antenna on the top of the north tower of the Lions Gate Bridge. From this location we could direct our programming exclusively to North and West Vancouver, using specially designed transmitting antennae.

Finding a suitable available frequency was the next big

hurdle. In Ottawa, the word was that no frequencies were available. I came up with a plan to utilize 107.1 MHZ, one of several unused frequencies reserved for Powell River, an area north of the Sunshine Coast. This meant our Squamish frequency of 104.9 MHZ could be moved to North Vancouver where it would not conflict with other signals. We received a letter from the federal ministry authorizing the move: Powell River to Squamish and Squamish to the North Shore. The letter ended with, "Good Luck" – I suppose with tongue in cheek.

No wonder the good luck wish. The cat was out of the bag. It didn't take long for Star FM, Chilliwack, to grasp the possible use of our Mountain FM 104.9 MHZ frequency in the Greater Vancouver area.

Star FM applied for a licence to cover Abbotsford, in the Fraser Valley east of Vancouver, knowing the signal would also reach Vancouver proper.

The CRTC hearing was called for our North Shore application, a 3,000-watt transmitter on the Lions Gate Bridge, and the Star FM application for a big 50,000-watt station in Abbotsford, where it would be in a position to invade the Vancouver market. We opposed the Star FM use of the Squamish frequency 104.9 MHZ because of the potential interference it would cause to our signal. The Star FM spokesperson called our opposition a "red herring – nothing to it at all."

I couldn't believe this blatant lie. My experience in our

mountainous corridor painted the picture for me. I could see what the Star FM's signal would do as clearly as if it were lightning dancing from mountain to mountain. Alas, what could a little bush station from the West tell the experts in Ottawa? And who was floating a red herring? Subsequently, Star FM did move into the Vancouver market.

Our application was denied. With the decision came disaster. Star FM, Abbotsford, went on the air with our hijacked frequency and immediately our Bowen Island transmitter was overtaken by the Star FM signal, effectively shutting down Mountain FM's broadcasting to the Sunshine Coast. If that wasn't enough, the Star FM signal seriously distorted our Squamish signal on the Sea to Sky Highway to West Vancouver. It was a major blow.

## *Different Problems*

Problems like these weren't solved in a day or a week. It took us months of lobbying, and costly engineering changes during which we were losing revenue. Weekends at home at the lake, when we could fit them in, became times to be treasured – more for a change of problems than relaxation.

What we had waiting at the lake was one of Canada's best-known bank robbers, although we didn't realize it at first. Our caretaker, Bill, a long, stringy cowboy type, had bamboozled us with a sheaf of forged references. It wasn't easy finding someone with the resourcefulness that we needed so we hired him without a qualm.

The subdivision water system and the electrical Pelton wheel had to be maintained. Bill tackled them with intelligence and gusto. He ran the bulldozer; the grounds, he told me, "would be like the grounds of the Parliament Buildings," and they were. He loved roses, bought and planted some. He was truly a find.

Bill also systematically took one item from our workshop every night to peddle at the Pemberton pub. I discovered this when my Suzuki, full to the gunwales with truck tires, was impounded one evening when Bill had encountered the RCMP on his way home. They were my extra set and Bill had been trying to sell them but didn't have any takers so he was bringing them home.

We had missed some other things earlier, but Bill had reported they were stolen by a thief who ran away with them after Bill caught him at work.

Later at the police station, the sergeant ran a check on our friend. We thought the information sheet would never end as it flowed and flowed from the computer.

Perhaps I should have been alerted when we watched a TV prison drama one evening with Bill. The prisoner character in the play was attempting to con the warden. The moment the warden succumbed to the bait, Bill rose from his chair shouting, "He took the hook, he took the hook!"

Meanwhile, the fight with Ottawa to restore Mountain

*Some of the Mountain FM on-air and creative personalities: Front left to right, Susan Johl, Rob Berridge, Diane Newman. Back left to right, David Larsen, Owen Searle, Darcy McCollom.*

FM coverage continued.

Listeners and merchants joined the Mountain FM battle, bombarding the CRTC with letters complaining about the loss of their local radio signal.

Our MLA, John Reynolds, MPs Lorne Greenaway and Mary Collins, and Senator Ray Perrault took up our cause, as did the members for the Sunshine Coast. The licensing authorities had made a big mistake; our prediction of a frequency conflict had been verified, but no progress was evident in restoring our unobstructed signal. In desperation, we offered to turn in our Sunshine Coast licences as we could no longer meet our legal broadcast requirements.

The solution to the Sea to Sky signal distortion finally came from the one I had presented for the North Shore application; the reserve Powell River frequency of 107.1 MHZ could be utilized in Squamish, the Squamish frequency of 104.9 MHZ would be relinquished to Star FM.

The Federal Business Development Bank and our shareholders were still hanging in there, supporting us. So, in Squamish, we installed a new antenna system broadcasting the new frequency 107.1 MHZ and we were back in business. And, so that we could recoup our position on the Sunshine Coast, the Ministry of Communications approved power increases for the Sunshine Coast stations.

## Playing with the Big Boys

However, the idea of extending our coverage to the North Shore just wouldn't go away.

The CRTC now knew Mountain FM and we had learned more about them. Encouragement coming from government sources and colleagues proved irresistible. We filed a second application for a North Shore licence.

I could feel the kiss of death in the room at the second hearing when I heard one CRTC official whispering, "I hate being part of this type of hearing." And it was unlike the first one; the big guns were now awakened and out to scuttle our application.

It was a foregone conclusion: the hearing was only to comply with the process, our application would again be denied. By now, Whistler was becoming a success story, promising a healthy market. The big broadcast groups were seeking a way to enter the beckoning market and didn't want a strong contender in the field.

The CKNW (WIC) group presented tough opposition, labelling us a little backwoods station. We had recently transferred our satellite feed facilities from their service to Selkirk Broadcasting. The change effectively cut out

Whistler exposure to CKNW, because they had commercial time as part of the feed package. We felt this was a major factor in their opposition, although they maintained Greater Vancouver couldn't handle another station vying for market revenue.

C-FUN, holding an AM licence only, wanted an FM licence for Vancouver and didn't want us complicating their chances, but stated they feared market reduction as well. Mountain FM was playing with the big boys. Our application was denied.

Over coffee sometime later with the CRTC hearing chairperson, whom I will not name, I asked the real reason our application was denied. The answer, "Well, we could not grant such a licence, the station could possibly become valuable." What crap! I thought we were in business to be successful. I guess our brash little station had to stay with marginal markets and wait its turn at the trough.

*Darcy McCollom, Creative Director, producing winning radio commercials.*

It is true that to be successful in most endeavours, the tide and wind has to be favourable. The concept was good and we gave it our best, but the timing wasn't right for Mountain FM. Certainly the argument that the market couldn't stand another station didn't wash. Shortly after, there were several new licences granted in the Vancouver area.

Happily, broadcasting wasn't all frequency squabbles and CRTC hearings. Positive things were happening in Mountain FM country. Interest in outdoor recreation of all kinds was

*Carol Roycroft, accounting, and Maureen Payette, traffic manager, competently handled the essential details in the front office.*

growing fast and the potential of the Sea to Sky corridor and the Sunshine Coast, so close to Vancouver, was unbeatable.

We settled down to do some growing of our own. The morning show with David Larsen at the helm and Diane Newman on news gained popularity. The Creative Department won awards for commercials, and sales and promotions were doing a fine job.

Traffic and Accounting switched to computers. Up to this time our traffic managers had, by hand, charted every single second of broadcast time, 24 hours a day, seven days a week. These logs were the menu of the day for the on-air crew. Logs were also a vital record for the CRTC to check in the event we had transgressed or deviated from our promise of performance.

Then one morning out of the blue, Carol woke up and announced, "It's time to sell Mountain FM. Radio is for young people and Lillooet Lake is calling."

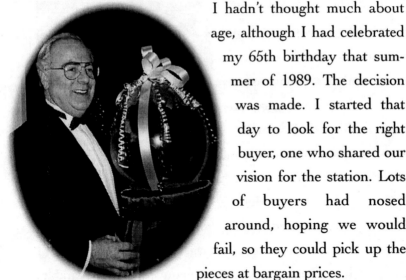

I hadn't thought much about age, although I had celebrated my 65th birthday that summer of 1989. The decision was made. I started that day to look for the right buyer, one who shared our vision for the station. Lots of buyers had nosed around, hoping we would fail, so they could pick up the pieces at bargain prices.

*Tom Peacock, General Manager, Selkirk Broadcasting, hosting 1989 Christmas party for CKSS-FM, CKWX and Mountain FM staff members.*

We had been happy doing business with Selkirk Broadcasting, providers of our satellite service and the parent company of CKSS and CKWX in Vancouver. Tom Peacock, their general manager, was a true gentleman and helpful associate in the business. The deal was soon struck: we would sell to Selkirk and stay on for a few months to help in the transition. Their engineering department would have to be acquainted with the idiosyncrasies of Mountain FM's seven mountaintop transmitters.

The radio business is all about change and before long, Selkirk Holdings, the parent of Selkirk Broadcasting, was transformed through several owners to become part of the Rogers Broadcasting network.

One of my last emergency repairs was on an icy New Year's Day. Carol and I boarded a helicopter at Whistler, to be landed at the mountaintop transmitter site. Flying over the valley, we could see below a panoramic Grandma Moses action scene: bright little figures at play, a spectacular picture of Whistler success.

The chopper deposited us on the snow, it was chillingly cold and the rotating blades blew up a miniature blizzard. We shovelled our way down to the split-level door of the transmitter building and thankfully were soon inside.

The trouble was at the receiving antenna on a mount at the edge of a cliff. Carol, fearing for my life, attached a rope around my waist, secured it around a tree and carefully let me down the icy slope. Up the short tower, I could work bare-handed for only about 60 seconds at a time in the freezing cold. Then I would have to warm my hands in my armpits.

The temperature was the problem. The cold had contracted the inner connector. I bent the pin for temporary repair. From our small test radio, music burst forth, over the mountain. And I felt the same thrill of years ago when I supplied radiotelephone communication to the B.C. coast.

It was tough to say farewell to the endeavour we had founded and devoted all our energy to for 10 years. On the other hand, the challenges of a changing Lillooet Lake were real. It was time to turn our attention home.

# CHAPTER 14
# CHANGES AT THE LAKE

It had all started in the early 70s when we wondered, what to do with this three-quarters of a mile of shorefront on Lillooet Lake? The mink ranch was being wound down and perhaps, we thought, a recreational subdivision. The lake had long ago captured my heart. Surely pioneering types would love it as well, perhaps enough to spend their summers without hydro power or (until much later, when we set up a water system) flush toilets.

It was months in the making. In the interim, we were pressured to accept orders for lakeshore property. The first customer was our good friend, Bill Forrest, a veterinarian who frequently visited us at the lake during the mink ranch days. He schooled us about mink medical procedures. One day, he handed me a cheque, asking for a prime waterfront lot and an agreement to purchase.

*Lake road washout not far from where huge boulder blocked road to lot buyers. This is my Suzuki used by bank robber Bill to make his daily stolen property runs from our shop.*

I was shoveling mink shit at the moment and said I couldn't take the time to write a formal agreement but if he wanted a receipt, I would give him one and promptly took out my pocket knife, cut a piece of birch bark from the nearest tree, wrote up an agreement with my mink marking pen, dated and signed it.

His lawyer ruled it a binding agreement, birch bark and all. Our friend framed it and in time got his lot.

Attempts to obtain subdivision approval were exhaustive and exhausting. We finally realized there would be no approval by the Department of Highways under the requirements of the day for "legal" access.

The forestry and Hydro road or industrial road, as it was referred to, did not qualify. There was access alright, but not access that met Department of Highways critera. But one plan caught the eye of the newly created Squamish-Lillooet Regional District. Slim Fougberg, the chairman, suggested a land-use contract for our proposed development. We vig-

*Aerial view of mill operation in 1977 showing planer mill, lumber piles ready for trucking, sawmill, shop, office and residence. Pelton wheel building and pipeline to dam on the right.*

orously pursued this idea, and with the legal representatives of the regional district, jointly prepared a draft contract.

The contract called for an on-site survey, done by land surveyor George Miller, depositing the land title in trust with Canada Trust, and establishing estate corporations for each developmental phase. Government ministries concerned would have to give approval.

At this stage we learned legislation had recently been passed terminating land-use contracts. Another scramble of phone calls and consultations, with a ruling that our development had been ongoing and a special order-in-council would be passed allowing us to go ahead. Our development was called Heather Jean Estates, after Heather, my daughter, and Jean, my late wife, who loved the property but did not live to see it enjoyed by our new Lillooet Lake enthusiasts.

275

*Slim Fougberg, Chairman of the Squamish Lillooet Regional District when Heather Jean Estates was created, and Margaret Fougberg, Pemberton historian and teacher on the main Street of Pemberton, July, 1981.*

## A Visit to the Dentist

To illustrate how critical matters were: the day before the order-in-council was to be passed, the government legal people realized they had no signature from Canada Trust. This necessitated my quick return to Vancouver from Victoria to track down the signing officer for Canada Trust. The officer was found seated in the dentist's chair with a rubber mask in his mouth. I read the document, held it on the dentist's tool tray, placed a pen in his hand and obtained the required signature. It was somewhat like a last-minute stay of execution.

I used the dental office phone to call Victoria and assured

the powers in charge that the document had been duly signed (no faxes then) by the trust company and witnessed by the dentist. The order was passed that day, March 3, 1977. Now we had only to wait for the formality of the land-use contract registration with the Kamloops Land Registry.

We were all set now to go ahead except for money. We figured the development work we could handle ourselves, if only we had a bulldozer. Our Vancouver bank manager looked at our plans, aerial and site photos. Getting no response to my request for a loan, I gathered my papers to leave.

"Put me down for the first lot No. 1, " he replied. "Here is my cheque and you have your loan too." Well as they say, we were off to the races. Twenty years later, we had the pleasure of finding a buyer for the bank manager's lot at many times the original price.

The initial lot sales were important because we needed the funds to go ahead with development work. My most important sale, though, had been made earlier, when I had been lucky enough to convince an attractive lot prospect that an easy, leisurely life in the country was right for her.

And so, Carol became my wife and joined me at the lake in the mid-'70s, understanding that ease and leisure were country words for hard work.

We roughed in road access to our first few properties and advertised in the Vancouver Sun. Replies came by radiotele-phone and a viewing date was set. It was mid-March and at

*Cutting rough lumber, Dixie Joe in centre by conveyor.*

Lillooet Lake, winter was over. Would you believe, our first sales campaign brought a freak snowstorm to the Pemberton area, making roads nearly impassable except on the lake road. Here we had no snow. Some of the eager buyers stayed in the hotel in Pemberton, others made it down the lake.

## We're Getting There

The lake was beautiful, the sun was shining, it was warm, in contrast to the surrounding areas. Our customers liked what they saw. Everyone was fed and bid good-bye. We had made eight sales to add to the bank manager's lot and a handful of Pemberton people who had bought ahead of the land-use contract.

But the day wasn't over – another problem. Kurt and Marlene Poetzschke, speaking for the convoy of cars about to climb the 30-per-cent grade at the head of the lake, returned to report the road was impassable. A rock the size of a car had rolled down the mountain, blocking the way. Off Bruce went to the rescue with our used Vickers bulldozer. Within a short time they were all on their way, very impressed with our rescue performance.

Bruce had been a sawyer at the Evans Products Sawmill in Pemberton. He was crazy about mills - making sawdust, as they say. His obsession soon led to a sawmill and planermill on the property. We supplied lumber to retailers Garibaldi Lumber, Curtis Lumber and Hollyburn Lumber, as well as Whistler builders. Heather Jean lot owners appreciated having on-site lumber, as the closest supply in those days was Squamish. We also offered cabin packages of small tongue-and-groove logs of our own design. We built several cabins for lot owners. Soon we were calling them Lou Logs and Lou Log Cabins.

*Heather Jean planer mill where rough lumber was planed smooth for market. Bruce and Lynn Potvin to the right.*

*Builders Garth Babcock and Dave Hemmingson working on a Heather Jean Lou Log Cabin.*

Operating the sawmill required a crew. Bruce and his wife Lynn did a good job of training inexperienced people, turning them into valuable skilled workers. Most of our crew were from the nearby Mount Currie Reserve, others were Vancouver youths under training programs. Expert mechanical people did part-time and emergency work. At one point half the workers in our crew were women. We also hired many transient workers, some of them very strange. One planerman arrived with his little dog Fifi. He had won the million-dollar lottery and had spent it all.

It was interesting to hear him tell what he did with the million dollars. Seems he gave a lot of it away, was conned out of some and spent the rest without regard for the future. The winner was Fifi, for whom we had to deduct from his paycheque the price of a large package of fresh liver and garlic cloves on a regular basis. That is not all – Fifi's liver had to be boiled and flavoured with the garlic. The former millionaire was really a very gentle and caring person.

Another fellow, from Nova Scotia, had served in the U.S. forces in Vietnam. He took great delight in recounting his gruesome experiences in the war. It seemed to have affected his mind somewhat, as he liked being armed. Carl was first hired as a cook, but the crew, not liking his soup or his kind, gave him a rough time.

He spent his time-off cleaning his guns and running a mail-order business dispensing information on the occult from a postal box number in Bellingham, across the U.S. border. But it was the soup and the fishcakes for breakfast that the crew disliked most.

One day he asked if he could work in the sawmill. He worked hard in the hot sun, piling lumber until 11:00 a.m., then came into the house upset and agitated at having been shown by Lynn, the supervisor, how to lever large beams into place. He said he couldn't take orders from a woman, so I drove him into Pemberton with cheque in hand.

## *A Busy Place*

Basically everyone did everything. At our busiest we ran two shifts a day, six days a week. Out-of-town workers lived in our bunkhouse and were fed in our home.

To transport workers back and forth to Mount Currie, we bought an old, well-used crummy, a sort of bus used to transport workers at logging camps. The old crummy box later had a second life as the Mountain FM transmitter building at the Pemberton site.

On a winter trip to Guatemala, we invited a friend to

*Eve Alvarez, friend and camp cook from Guatemala, holding Chinook salmon from the lake. The salmon is big but Eve doesn't quite make 5 feet in height.*

come and cook for the mill crew. With no spoken English, Eve was a big favourite for two summers. Spanish became the mealtime language, with Eve reigning supreme. We had jokes and laughter over our efforts to communicate. Communication must have been achieved because Eve soon had serious admirers.

The lumber market collapsed in the early '80s and we closed the mill. The good days were over and just like the mink ranch, the mill was no longer compatible with a growing recreational subdivision. Bruce and Lynn moved on to Mount Currie to start a new mill endeavour known as Creekside Forest Products.

After several years, Bruce was injured in a serious mill accident and his impaired health put an end to their business. At their peak, they could not keep up with the mill orders, most for the export market. Obtaining saw logs in the middle of a forest area is another story too long to tell.

I am frequently stopped on the street in Pemberton by former mill workers who tell me how much they miss those days, and ask how Bruce is doing.

The Heather Jean Properties development needed a water system; Cataline Creek (named after a famed Gold Rush mule train packer) ran through the property. Jack Sunell, a water engineer, was engaged to come up with a design to serve the subdivision. Approvals and permits were applied for and granted. We commenced laying 6" "Blue Brute" pipelines. We purchased a backhoe and I polished up my blasting ticket.

So once again, it was off to the bank, this time the Federal Business Development Bank, then the bank of last resort. Several loans were taken out over the next few years starting out at 9 per cent interest, rising to 22 per cent. Having guaranteed the lot owners a fixed water fee for 15 years, we had a tight management situation. In times like these, one appreciates the value of the government bank. We might ask where are the commercial banks when needed? Oh yes, they are there when the real need has diminished and returns are guaranteed.

We laid over 2 miles of water line through the nothing-but-rock mountainside, doing the work ourselves. We installed wooden-stave water storage tanks using a pickle-tank design from southern Ontario.

Some surprising things occurred when we were blasting for the water line trench. We had to take cover to dodge flying rocks, and one time, after notices were posted and alarms sounded, out walked a fellow from the bush towards the water trench. We shouted to him and received a good-natured wave in return. He thought World War III had started when multiple blasts went off all at once.

We hoped blasting would rid us of mosquitoes. It turned out the clouds of mosquitoes merely got blown upwards, descending a few moments later to resume their feeding frenzy. Birds seemed to wait about one minute to start chirping again.

## We Created a Community

When the lakeshore lots were all sold, we developed sites further back from the lakeshore and provided common lot areas for all to use for lake access. In time, all the 152 lots were spoken for and the lot owners formed a new team to manage their interests, now known as Lillooet Lake Estates Ltd.

As the sites began to fill up, Carol and I worried about the Heather Jean subdivision attracting motorcycle gangs or becoming a hideaway for heavy drinking parties. We were determined to preserve it as a quiet family retreat.

So I was disturbed one Saturday morning when two helmeted bikers drove up our driveway and asked about property. Our minds were made up that there would be no sale to these tough guys, so I was not too informative.

But as time passed, they took off their helmets and I realized they both spoke nicely and seemed to be regular guys. One turned out to be the fire chief of Surrey and, right on the spot, he bought a lot from Carol.

Chief Al Cleaver and his wife Connie became good friends of ours over the years, and our mill supplied the lumber for "The Barn," the cottage they built themselves. Their neighbours Vince and Louise Holmes, Vancouver business people, also became good friends and bought one of our economy Lou Log cedar tongue-and-groove homes.

They later upgraded it into a small palace and named it "The Holmestead."

In October 1984, we had the once-in-200-years Pemberton Valley flood. The Lillooet River overflowed its banks, breaking through dikes into farmland and inundating parts of the town and highway.

At the head of Lillooet Lake, the water covered our only road access to Pemberton and Squamish. At home, our dock was under five feet of water but, incredibly, the Pelton wheel kept turning over, ever so slowly, under 18 inches of water.

Anxious to get back to our radio station in Squamish, 70 miles away, we hopped into the truck as soon as the water started to recede. The river was still flowing over a wide area of the road at the head of the lake, but we had long ago worked out a routine for driving through high water.

Carol walked ahead of the truck with a pole, probing the depth of the water and testing to see if the road was still intact while I drove behind. This division of labour was by mutual consent; Carol was a swimmer and preferred to be swept away by the current, while I, a non-swimmer, felt safer being swept away in a container, if indeed it came to that.

We made our way several hundred feet to a small hump of dry roadbed where we were greeted surprisingly by two large pink pigs, presumably washed down by the river. We continued into the water ahead, Carol picking her way with a pig swimming on either side, snuffling and snorting in delight to have company.

Finally we reached dry land and the road ahead. Carol climbed into the truck and, sadly, had to leave the pigs squealing at her heels.

The lake and the subdivision weren't our only worries in the '80s. Mountain FM, our radio broadcasting venture, was struggling. But the economic slump had killed property sales and our mill was "no more" so we were able to leave the lake in the hands of caretakers while we spent most of our time in Squamish, running the radio station.

Our best caretakers were Peter and Teresa Han from Korea, who were preparing for their future as missionaries in Africa. They performed their duties well, translated Biblical tracts in their free time and offered cheerful company on our days at home.

# CHAPTER 15
# LET THERE BE LIGHT

Every necessity at the lake had to be carted in by hand, by train to Mount Currie then jeeped through the reserve and down the old hydro road to the lake, 15 miles of rocky punishment. Items which had been destined for the Salvation Army became treasures for our pioneer hideaway. We lovingly transported everything: worn-out furniture, cabinets, toasters, old lamps and other small appliances.

Friends at work questioned my judgment when it came to the electrical stuff. We had no hydro and no prospects for future service, and even now, 40-odd years later, we have no hydro. Their suggestion that natural beauty and primitive living go hand-in-hand caused me to reflect: What did I want, what was I doing and where was it all going? Setting my priorities was simple. Achieving them would take more than a quick, introspective assessment.

First, the lake was a family retreat, a place the children could enjoy in the summer and weekends and where the adults could unwind. We were not purists, we enjoyed nature but felt there was no requirement that we live in a primitive manner. Why not combine the mountain beauty with modern comforts? However, I found trying to meet our comfort level through methods from the past cost more than establishing a source of electrical power from the start. Besides, coal oil and gas lamps were a fire hazard. You can't beat a wood-burning stove for cozy, fast warmth but it is no sin to maintain residual heat from electric or propane heaters.

## Wind and Water

Before we came to these conclusions I experimented with a wind charger with a 10-foot wooden propeller. The unit had come from an old farm in Manitoba and cost all of $50. It generated 32 volts DC (direct current) under a strong wind and you were safe so long as the wooden propeller didn't disintegrate.

Prairie wind chargers of the old days were all 32-volt DC. Farmers looking for generators were sold off-the-shelf units used in trains. Each railway passenger car used a 32-volt generator to charge a set of batteries, which stored electricity for use when the car was stationary. With some adaptations, prairie farmers used wind-driven 32-volt lighting for years.

*The small mountain lake in foreground feeds the creek which provides water for our dam and Pelton wheel. Lillooet Lake in background to the right.*
*Photo by Margaret Brown*

Many small coastal logging camps used 32-volt DC gas-powered generators for operating radiotelephones and charging the batteries. Again, a carryover from railcars and coastal vessels.

But during our second summer, the wind didn't blow and the wind charger was dismantled. Fear of someone being killed by the propeller was also a strong deciding factor. Hauling 45-gallon drums of gas to run the 32-volt Briggs and Stratton generator now consumed my weekends. With the battery storage of power, we had lights and could call out on the radiotelephone and ham station. However, I lacked the few personal priorities of my life, toaster, sandwich maker, power tools and broadcast radio receiver, all needing 115 volts. And so, the next step, when we could

*The first Pelton wheel building on the lakeshore. Aluminum pipe carries water from dam 1100 feet away. The land is just beginning to recover from the logging activities in the 1940's and early 1950's.*

afford it, was a 115-volt AC (alternating current) generating plant, which could also charge batteries. We restored nighttime and emergency light but still the labour and cost of hauling gasoline were considerable.

A friend at work asked about water power. Immediately, the light came on; I remembered the Pelton wheels on the coast. Jack Tindall had one at Refuge Cove. Would it be possible to generate power from our small creek? I headed for the library to study the scant information available.

A Pelton wheel is a small, enclosed metal wheel with eggcup-like appendages welded on the circumference. A jet of water hits the cups, thereby rotating the wheel. Creek water is stored in a dam at the proper elevation and distance, providing a steady flow down a pipeline to the wheel, which rotates the generator. Simple.

I started a search for a wheel. None were to be found at first. Discouraged, but still determined, one noon-hour's browsing around a metal scrap yard yielded the object of my desire lying in a heap of trash metal, price: $10. We emptied

our piggy banks and pur-
chased a war surplus gen-
erator to complete the
package, cost: $100
American.

In 1966, we were gener-
ating 5,000 watts, meeting
all our electrical needs.
During the mink ranch
days we found a second
wheel to generate power
for a walk-in freezer used
for mink food storage.

*Pelton wheel as it is today. Wayne Ferguson performing a regular maintenance check.*

*More Power to Us*

Today, with still no prospect of hydro service at the lake, our system generates 16,000 watts, 120/240 volts, enabling modern conveniences in a rustic lakeshore environment. Our newly built cabins on the family property employ today's solar technology with a shot of Pelton wheel power for battery charging during winter months.

Self-sufficiency in the bush, especially self-sufficiency of power, is a dream of many. It was once thought of as con-quering nature but truly it is working with nature to provide your needs. Many who shared the dream, also shared their knowledge with me. The library provided formulas for

291

water flow and generating capacity. I was fortunate to have been in the right place over the years to develop some skills to act on this knowledge.

However, traditional trial and error was still part of the process. Our first dam was constructed of logs but, of course, they had to be put in place. Charlie Mack Seymour from Mount Currie came to the rescue. After all, the Indians had been moving huge logs without machines for hundreds of years. So that is what Charlie did.

The log dam worked but not well enough; too much water escaped and too much sand and gravel filled the dam pool. It had to be concrete, with the basic features of a major hydro installation.

I designed these features, the bottom drain for self-clean-

*Members of the Point Grey Ham Club inspecting the new*
*Heather Jean dam under construction in May 1995.*
*The old dam made of concrete mixed by hand, pail by pail,*
*worked perfectly for over 30 years.*

ing, overflow channel and filter box, tailored to our particular creek after daily and year-round study. Every water course has its own individual characteristics which have to be taken into account. Then, I allowed for the unpredictable which is predictable.

When everything was in place we poured the concrete, one-half of the dam at a time, diverting the water around the site. Conscripted family members mixed the cement by hand and carried it to the site in pails. No dawdling was permitted because we needed an even pour for strength.

Whenever I hear the sound of small streams splashing against the rocks, churning their way down to the lake, I have a feeling of awe realizing the potential of the kinetic energy before my eyes. It is plain magic to harness a small stream of water, have it turn a wheel, rotate a generator and convert the water flow into heat, cold, rotating devices, television, communications and, above all, light.

Our hand-poured dam lasted 32 years before being replaced by a new beauty constructed of concrete delivered by a cement truck.

# Chapter 16
# Sans Regrets

In the last few years, the action at Louis' Place on the lake has quietened down, but, like life itself, it still goes on.

It has been a real challenge for me, a grade eight dropout, to write about myself. I had to learn the lessons of life as I advanced, step by step. I taught myself to write about electronic products and make business proposals, but writing about myself brought me face to face with who I am and what I have done with my life.

My mother told me I would have good fortune because of the veil, or caul, over my head when I was born, and who knows if there is anything to that old superstition? But I do know she taught me the power of positive thinking.

So here we are, running at a slower pace in this beautiful place.

We have been building cabins for friends and family

members along the lakeshore.

We have welcomed a new daughter-in-law, Aya, into the family and watched the total of grandchildren grow to 12, and it is a delight to watch them develop.

And, on long summer days, we often cruise the lake with friends on our houseboat, the Carolou, which we trucked in through the rock cut at the head of the lake with only an inch or two to spare. It is now housed in a rock-basket boat basin which we built when the water level was low.

At times we have been cut off from the outside world: by heavy snows – I had to hike in on snowshoes (it took me 11 hours from the head of the lake) with a heavy pack of groceries during the big winter of 1967 – and by floods – when the lake rose so high the houseboat floated over the rock baskets and onto the lawn. A couple of times it meant a helicopter trip out.

But we have enjoyed it all, and, for now, farewell from our place at the lake:

AU REVOIR
HASTA LUEGO
SAYONARA
さようなら

# LOUIS' PLACE
## ORDERING INFORMATION

Louis' Place recollects many experiences, from rural Alberta to Port Coquitlam BC, from the Canadian Air Force to flying the BC Coast. From Japan to Cuba, to a recreational paradise on Lillooet Lake and the creation of Mountain FM.

This book has come about at the urging of many, and not produced without its share of blood, sweat and tears!

Should you not find a copy at your local bookstore, I would be pleased to mail one or more to you, or to someone on your behalf. The cost is $27.95 CDN plus $5.00 postage & handling or $19.95 US plus $3.50 postage & handling.

Please send orders with payment and mailing instructions to:

Carolou, Box 220, Pemberton, BC Canada.

Book Stores and agents may order from the publisher, toll-free (Canada and USA) 1-888-232-4444, e-mail: bookstore@trafford.com

ISBN 155212293-X

9 781552 122938